"These authors delight in t
try, which beautifully accer
the Gospel abounds with an................al wisdom for every generation.
It isn't just a book for pastors but for everyone who needs, knows,
loves, and proclaims the gospel of Jesus Christ. God has entrusted every
Christian with the glorious ministry of his abundant life-giving gospel,
but like Timothy, many Christians are timid and lack confidence and
wisdom in their efforts to herald the gospel entrusted to them. This
book offers a much needed clarion call to gospel-established ministry
for the church at the beginning of the twenty-first century."

Burk Parsons, Associate Minister, St. Andrew's Chapel, Sanford,
FL; editor, _Tabletalk_

"Every minister of the gospel would be wise to reflect carefully and
prayerfully on 2 Timothy. The esteemed contributors to this volume
will help you do just that with insightful biblical exegesis, discernment of pressing contemporary challenges, and love for Christ and his
church."

Collin Hansen, _Christianity Today_ editor-at-large and author of
_Young, Restless, Reformed: A Journalist's Journey with the
New Calvinists_

"There are seasons of pastoral work in which the faithful shepherd
faces serious challenges, and at these times he longs for words of
refreshment, wisdom, encouragement, power, and endurance. These six
expositions of Paul's last charge to his suffering protégé provide a shot
in the arm to stir both weary and strong shepherds to greater faithfulness in the ministry trust given to them by Christ. They are sober and
sound catharses for the overseer's soul. Through these sermons you
hear the Spirit reminding you with joy, 'Rely on me so that you can stay
in the game with diligence until the end!'"

Eric C. Redmond, Senior Pastor, Reformation Alive Baptist
Church, Temple Hills, MD

"Piper, Ryken, Driscoll, Copeland, Chapell, and Duncan are very different people, but they are all proven champions of the unchanging gospel of Jesus. This book will help all Christians study to be faithful to the task we have been entrusted with to spread that same message. Paul's advice to his young apprentice Timothy is ably explained in these pages. Do your family, friends, and fellow church members a favor—read this book and apply it."

Adrian Warnock, author, *Raised With Christ*

"What you hold in your hands is a diversity of approaches to expositional preaching by some of today's most capable expositors who model the unity of the one gospel, applied by one man (Paul), in one context (the church in Ephesus), written to one pastor (Timothy). And because all Scripture is inspired by God and profitable, I am certain that you will profit from these expositions as you apply this one gospel, presented in 2 Timothy, to your own ministry context and your personal life."

Juan R. Sanchez, Jr., Preaching Pastor, High Pointe Baptist Church, Austin, TX

ENTRUSTED WITH THE GOSPEL

THE GOSPEL COALITION

The Gospel Coalition is a fellowship of evangelical churches deeply committed to renewing our faith in the gospel of Christ and to reforming our ministry practices to conform fully to the Scriptures. We have become deeply concerned about some movements within traditional evangelicalism that seem to be diminishing the church's life and leading us away from our historic beliefs and practices. On the one hand, we are troubled by the idolatry of personal consumerism and the politicization of faith; on the other hand, we are distressed by the unchallenged acceptance of theological and moral relativism. These movements have led to the easy abandonment of both biblical truth and the transformed living mandated by our historic faith. We not only hear of these influences, we see their effects. We have committed ourselves to invigorating churches with new hope and compelling joy based on the promises received by grace alone through faith alone in Christ alone.

We believe that in many evangelical churches a deep and broad consensus exists regarding the truths of the gospel. Yet we often see the celebration of our union with Christ replaced by the age-old attractions of power and affluence, or by monastic retreats into ritual, liturgy, and sacrament. What replaces the gospel will never promote a mission-hearted faith anchored in enduring truth working itself out in unashamed discipleship eager to stand the tests of kingdom calling and sacrifice. We desire to advance along the King's highway, always aiming to provide gospel advocacy, encouragement, and education so that current- and next-generation church leaders are better equipped to fuel their ministries with principles and practices that glorify the Savior and do good to those for whom he shed his life's blood.

We want to generate a unified effort among all peoples—an effort that is zealous to honor Christ and multiply his disciples, joining in a true coalition for Jesus. Such a biblically grounded and united mission is the only enduring future for the church. This reality compels us to stand with others who are stirred by the conviction that the mercy of God in Jesus Christ is our only hope of eternal salvation. We desire to champion this gospel with clarity, compassion, courage, and joy—gladly linking hearts with fellow believers across denominational, ethnic, and class lines.

Our desire is to serve the church we love by inviting all of our brothers and sisters to join us in an effort to renew the contemporary church in the ancient gospel of Christ so that we truly speak and live for him in a way that clearly communicates to our age. We intend to do this through the ordinary means of his grace: prayer, the ministry of the Word, baptism and the Lord's Supper, and the fellowship of the saints. We yearn to work with all who, in addition to embracing the confession and vision set out here, seek the lordship of Christ over the whole of life with unabashed hope in the power of the Holy Spirit to transform individuals, communities, and cultures.

ENTRUSTED WITH THEGOSPEL

Pastoral Expositions of 2 Timothy

by John Piper, Philip Ryken, Mark Driscoll, K. Edward Copeland,
Bryan Chapell, J. Ligon Duncan

Edited by
D. A. Carson

CROSSWAY
WHEATON, ILLINOIS

Library of Congress Cataloging-in-Publication Data
Gospel Coalition, National Conference (2009 : Chicago, IL)
   Entrusted with the Gospel : pastoral expositions of 2 Timothy / edited by D. A. Carson.
      p. cm.
Includes index.
   ISBN 978-1-4335-1583-5 (tpb)
   1. Bible. N.T. Timothy, 2nd—Criticism, interpretation, etc.—Congresses.
I. Carson, D. A. II. Title.
BS2745.52.G67   2010
227'.840601—dc22   2010010231

CONTENTS

PREFACE

D. A. Carson

For the national conference of The Gospel Coalition, held in Chicago in April 2009, the planners decided that at least eight of the nine plenaries had to be expositions of Scripture. The additional plenary address was delivered by Ajith Fernando from Sri Lanka, whom we asked to give us a more global vision, an outside-North-America vision, of the strengths and weaknesses of confessional evangelicalism. His talk was both moving and challenging, and was itself deeply anchored in Scripture. Of the eight expositions, the planners devoted six to the unpacking of one New Testament book, 2 Timothy. That book was particularly appropriate for two reasons—first, it has a great deal to say about the gospel; and second, it is particularly pertinent to young pastors and would-be pastors, many of whom attended the conference while another twenty-five thousand or so followed online.

We are profoundly grateful to God for the outcome. Many conferences these days emphasize exposition of Scripture, and rightly so, for we do not live by bread alone, but by every word that proceeds from the mouth of God. To expound all of one biblical book in one conference, however, added another dimension—the integration provided by one document, by the study of one sustained New Testament letter. Perhaps equally important was the diversity of styles exemplified by the six preachers. Someone has said that if you listen to only one preacher all the time, you will become a clone; if you listen to two, you will become confused; if you listen to many, you are on the threshold of becoming wise and of growing into your own style. (It is not for nothing that Phillips Brooks said that preaching is truth *through human personality*.) The best of expository preaching takes its message and its thrust, and, ideally, even its form, from the biblical text itself. Most of our preachers managed this superbly while remaining, in form and style, exceedingly diverse. So let wisdom grow and stylistic freedom reign.

Some of the sermons were delivered from a full manuscript; others were not. All of the preachers graciously took the time to provide, after the fact, a full text. For this volume, these were capably read and commented on by Andy Naselli, to whom my debt grows month by month. Although the videos of the sermons as they were preached are available on the Coalition's Web site (www.thegospelcoalition.org), many people want the printed form provided by this book, either because they prefer it or because the printed word is conducive to meditative pauses, underlining, and praying over what is being learned.

So we are very grateful to Crossway for aiding and abetting the Coalition in circulating this exposition of 2 Timothy.

1

FEED THE FLAME OF GOD'S GIFT: UNASHAMED COURAGE IN THE GOSPEL

(2 Timothy 1:1–12)

John Piper

Paul, an apostle of Christ Jesus by the will of God according to the promise of the life that is in Christ Jesus,

To Timothy, my beloved child:

Grace, mercy, and peace from God the Father and Christ Jesus our Lord.

I thank God whom I serve, as did my ancestors, with a clear conscience, as I remember you constantly in my prayers night and day. As I remember your tears, I long to see you, that I may be filled with joy. I am reminded of your sincere faith, a faith that dwelt first in your grandmother Lois and your mother Eunice and now, I am sure, dwells in you as well. For this reason I remind you to fan into flame the gift of God, which is in you through the laying on of my hands, for God gave us a spirit not of fear but of power and love and self-control.

Therefore do not be ashamed of the testimony about our Lord, nor of me his prisoner, but share in suffering for the gospel by the power of God, who saved us and called us to a holy calling, not because of our works but because of his own purpose and grace, which he gave us in Christ Jesus before the ages began, and which now has been manifested through the appearing of our Savior Christ Jesus, who abolished death and brought life and immortality to light through the gospel, for which I was appointed a preacher and apostle and teacher, which is why I suffer as I do. But I am not ashamed, for I know whom I have believed, and I am convinced that he is able to guard until that Day what has been entrusted to me.

2 Tim. 1:1–12

I'll begin by trying to put in my own words the main point of this passage, that is, the point that everything else in this passage supports or explains. I'll say it as though I was Paul and you were Timothy. In fact, I will deliver almost this entire message as though I was Paul and you were Timothy. The main point of this passage goes like this:

> Timothy, keep feeding the white-hot flame of God's gift—of unashamed courage to speak openly of Christ and to suffer for the gospel.

FEED THE FLAME!

Feed it, Timothy. Feed it. Feed this flame! Because if you don't, it will go out. Don't quench this spirit, Timothy. It is a gift from God. Fan it till it is white-hot. Feed it till it is all ablaze. Everything else in this passage serves to explain and empower that feeding, that gift, that courage, that speaking and suffering for that gospel. *Timothy, keep feeding the white-hot flame of God's gift—of unashamed courage to speak openly of Christ and to suffer for the gospel.*

Here's where we're going with this main point. First, we will see where it comes from in the text. Second, we will see that it's the burden of the whole book, not just this paragraph. Third, we will see how Paul intends for this feeding the flame of God's gift to happen. And fourth, we will do it, that is, I will take Paul's fuel and, by the Spirit, try to feed the flame of God's gift in your life.

The Main Point in This Text

The text's main point is found in verses 6–8:

> *For this reason I remind you to fan into flame the gift of God, which is in you through the laying on of my hands, for God gave us a spirit not of fear but of power and love and self-control.*

Therefore do not be ashamed of the testimony about our Lord, nor of me his prisoner, but share in suffering for the gospel by the power of God. . . .

Timothy, keep feeding the white-hot flame. . . . This comes from verse 6, "I remind you to fan into flame. . . ." The imagery of fire and flame is not mine. It's Paul's. He says, "Fan into *flame*. . . ."

WHITE-HOT

All I add to this is a few words, like "white-hot," to bring out two things. First, fire is hot. Really hot. There is hot, and then there is *hot*. You might say, "I've got a fever. I'm really hot." Well, you're not really hot. I can touch your forehead, and it doesn't burn me. But if you light a bonfire, and I stick my hand in it—that's hot. It's white-hot.

This is the way Paul talks in Romans 12:11—"Do not be slothful in zeal, *boil in spirit*" (translation mine). Paul wants Timothy *boiling*. He wants him *aflame*. Not fever-hot, but fire-hot—white-hot. Jesus spits lukewarm ministers out of his mouth (Rev. 3:16). So I use the words "white-hot flame" to make that clear.

KEEP FEEDING

Second, I add the phrase "keep feeding." Timothy, *keep feeding* the white-hot flame. The reason for this is that Paul's point is not that Timothy has grown cool and needs one good hot fix. That is not the point. The present tense for the verb "fan into flame" (verse 6, *anazōpurein*) is continuous, ongoing action.

So *Timothy, keep feeding the white-hot flame.* . . . Feed it. Feed it. Flames go out without continuous fuel.

THE GIFT OF GOD

Now, what is it that is supposed to be burning? What is aflame? What is to be kept burning? Verse 6 gives the answer. It's the gift that God has given Timothy. "For this reason I remind you to fan into flame *the gift of God." Timothy, keep feeding the white-hot flame of God's gift. . . .*

God gave a gift to Timothy. That gift includes fire. The ongoing existence of that fire is dependent on Timothy's obedience to verse 6. Feed it, Timothy. Fan it into flame over and over again. It will go out if you don't—even though it's the gift of God.

And lest you think at this point that God is held hostage to Timothy's weakness and can't make the gifts he gave him successful in blessing his church and reaching the lost, remember, *Timothy's fanning this gift into flame is also God's gift.* God makes the flame of his gifts dependent on our feeding, and then makes our feeding dependent on his grace. We will see this very shortly in the text.

Timothy, keep feeding the white-hot flame of God's gift—of unashamed courage to speak openly of Christ and to suffer for the gospel. I get the words "unashamed courage" from verses 7–8. Start in the middle of verse 6, ". . . the gift of God, which is in you through the laying on of my hands, for God gave us *a spirit not of fear* but of power and love and self-control. Therefore *do not be ashamed. . . ."*

COURAGE TO SUFFER FOR THE GOSPEL

God gave—that's a gift—a spirit *not of fear* but the opposite, *courage.* To be sure, powerful courage and loving courage and self-controlled courage—but the note falls on *courage* because verse 8 continues, "Therefore do not be ashamed. . . ." That's what courage is—it is not ashamed.

And specifically this unashamed courage is for what? Verse 8, "Therefore do not be ashamed of *the testimony about our Lord*, nor of me his prisoner, but *share in suffering for the gospel.*" Don't be ashamed of speaking openly about Christ, and don't be ashamed of the shameful circumstances of those who do—like my imprisonment. And don't be ashamed to suffer for the gospel.

On the contrary, verse 8 says, "Share in suffering for the gospel." Embrace this. God has given you this gift, Timothy—to burn with the courage to speak and to suffer. Feed that flame, Timothy. Feed it.

BY THE POWER OF GOD

Notice the last phrase of verse 8, "by the power of God." When all your feeding and fanning is done and your flame burns brightly and you speak boldly and suffer valiantly, who did it, Timothy? Where did this come from? God did it. You did it "by God's power." You acted, but his power was the decisive cause.

Unashamed speaking for Christ, courageous suffering with Christ, is by the power of God in Christ. Just like the disciples in Acts 4:31—"They were all filled with the Holy Spirit and continued to speak the word of God with boldness." No one can even say, "Jesus is Lord," except by the power of the Holy Spirit (1 Cor. 12:3)—let alone say it in the Coliseum or in Afghanistan or the university classroom.

THROUGH THE LAYING ON OF MY HANDS

How did Timothy get this gift of *unashamed courage to speak openly of Christ and to suffer for the gospel*? Paul says in verse 6 that he got it "through the laying on of my hands." "For this reason I remind you to fan into flame the gift of God, *which is in you through the laying on of my hands.*" In 1 Timothy 4:14, Paul says, "Do not neglect the gift you have, which was given you by prophecy when the council of elders laid their hands on you." I think Paul is referring to the same occasion.

So I picture it like this—as Timothy was being set apart for the ministry of the gospel, Paul and the elders were laying their hands on him and praying, and the Holy Spirit moved Paul to say this prophetic word, "Timothy, in answer to our prayers, God is going to give you a flaming unashamed courage for Christ beyond anything you've known."

TIMOTHY'S TEARS

At that moment, I imagine Timothy breaking down in tears and weeping. The reason I picture this is verse 4. It says, "As I remember your tears, I long to see you, that I may be filled with joy." Most commentators, it seems, think that these were tears of farewell, when Paul parted with Timothy. Nobody knows for sure. Still, why would we guess farewell tears when the main event of Timothy's life in this paragraph is the enormously powerful moment of the laying on of hands, and having God Almighty, through one of the most authoritative people on the planet, speak over your life, "Young man, against all your predilections and all your weaknesses and all your timidity, you will speak for me unashamedly and courageously, and you will suffer for my gospel"? I have prayed that perhaps God would do this for some of you right now. That God would take away the spirit of fear and give a spirit of unashamed courage to speak and suffer for Christ. In the name of Jesus, Father, do it.

So there it is. That's the main point of the paragraph and where I get it. *Timothy, keep feeding the white-hot flame of*

God's gift—of unashamed courage to speak openly of Christ and to suffer for the gospel.

The Burden of the Whole Book—Not Just This Paragraph

Now let the weight of this point sink in as you hear Paul underline it fourteen times in this little letter. It is not marginal. It is central. Paul wrote this letter for Timothy—and for you—because the flame of unashamed courage in us is always being smothered by the deadly, seemingly innocent pleasures of this world. May the Lord make this litany of unashamed courage in suffering feed the flame of courage in you:

> **1:16:** "Onesiphorus . . . was not ashamed of my chains."
> **2:3:** "Share in suffering as a good soldier of Christ Jesus."
> **2:9:** "I am suffering [for the gospel], bound with chains as a criminal."
> **2:10:** "I endure everything for the sake of the elect."
> **2:12:** "If we endure, we will also reign with him."
> **2:15:** "Do your best to present yourself . . . a worker who has no need to be ashamed."
> **2:24:** "And the Lord's servant must . . . patiently endur[e] evil."
> **3:1:** "In the last days there will come times of difficulty."
> **3:10–11:** "You . . . have followed my . . . persecutions and sufferings."
> **3:12:** "All who desire to live a godly life in Christ Jesus will be persecuted."
> **4:5:** "As for you . . . endure suffering."
> **4:6:** "I am already being poured out as a drink offering, and the time of my departure has come."
> **4:7:** "I have fought the good fight."
> **4:16:** "At my first defense no one came to stand by me, but all deserted me."

If you want an easy life, secure, esteemed, untroubled, comfortable, safe, then get out of the ministry of Christ. And if you are single, don't marry a woman who wants that. "If anyone would come after me, let him deny himself and take up his cross and follow me. For whoever would save his life will lose it, but whoever loses his life for my sake and the gospel's will save it" (Mark 8:34–35). The Calvary Road is a hard road, and the most joyful road of all—in the power of God.

How to Feed the Flame

Timothy, keep feeding the white-hot flame of God's gift—of unashamed courage to speak openly of Christ and to suffer for the gospel.

So, how does Paul mean for Timothy to feed this flame? He tells him to do it. Does he show him how? We have already seen part of the answer—the last phrase of verse 8 is "by the power of God." The flame of your unashamed courage to speak and suffer for Christ is sustained "by the power of God." You are given a spirit of power, love, and self-control.

So the question is, how does Timothy go on feeding the flame with this power? It's *God's* power. What do we do to experience the fullness of God's power for courage to suffer? You'll see one of the normative ways it works by making a connection between 2 Timothy 2:1 and 1:2. This is a key.

THE GRACE THAT IS IN JESUS

In 2:1, Paul answers our question, "You then, my child, *be strengthened* [be empowered] by the grace that is in Christ Jesus." So the power of verse 8 that sustains the fire of unashamed courage is "by the *grace* that is in Christ Jesus our Lord." So we trace the flame of unashamed courage back to the power of God in verse 8 and then back to the grace of God in 2:1. "Be strengthened [that is, feed the flaming power of God for courage] by the grace of God that is in Christ Jesus."

So how do you do that? How does Paul do that for Timothy? Now make the connection with 1:2. Watch for the word "grace" and how it functions, "To Timothy, my beloved child: *Grace*, mercy, and peace from God the Father and Christ Jesus our Lord." Timothy, grace to you. *Grace* to you!

GRACE TO YOU—GRACE BE WITH YOU

To get the force of this, it helps to notice something—every single letter that Paul writes, without exception, all thirteen of them, begins with some form of the words "grace *to you*." And every single one of them ends with some form of the words "grace be *with you*." There are no exceptions, including 2 Timothy 4:22—"The Lord be with your spirit. Grace be with you."

Why is it always "grace *to you*" at the beginning of the letters and "grace be *with you*" at the end of the letters? Here's my answer—because, as the letters begin, Paul believes that God's grace is being mediated to the readers by the words, the truth, of each letter. And as the letters end, and people have been receiving grace through reading or hearing these truths, he knows that the readers will now leave and return to the troubles of the world, and he prays that this grace, which they have now received through the Word of God, will go *with* them.

THROUGH THE WORD OF GOD

In other words, if you ask Paul, "How do I *feed the white-hot flame of God's gift of unashamed courage to speak openly of Christ and to suffer for the gospel*?" he answers, "*By the power of God*" (verse 8)—the supernatural power of the Holy Spirit. And if you ask, "How do I express the fullness of this power?" he answers in 2:1, "*Be strengthened by the grace that is in Christ Jesus.*" And if you ask him, "How do I receive this ongoing grace?" he answers, "*Timothy, this grace is coming to you right now through the Word of God.*" God's grace is coming to you in my words. "Now we have received not the spirit of the world, but the Spirit who is from God, that we might understand the things freely given us by God. And we impart this in words not taught by human wisdom but taught by the Spirit" (1 Cor. 2:12–13).

These aren't ordinary words, Timothy. They are God's words. You were with me on the beach in Miletus. Do you remember what I said as I left? I said, "I commend you to God and to *the word of his grace*, which is powerful to build you up [in courage!] and to give you the inheritance among all those who are sanctified" (Acts 20:32).

The answer, Timothy, is that you *feed the white-hot flame of unashamed courage to suffer for the gospel* by preaching to yourself the foundational truths of this letter. And you feed the courage of your people the same way. God has ordained that his sovereign grace comes to you with power for unashamed courage through my God-given words.

THE PROMISE OF LIFE IN JESUS

That was the point of verse 1, Timothy. I am "Paul, an apostle of Christ Jesus by the will of God according to the promise of the life that is in Christ Jesus." I am Christ's authorized spokesman. I was called to this by the will of God. I did not put myself in this position.

And my authority to speak on his behalf does not have a random focus. It focuses on "the promise of the life that is in Christ Jesus." You have this life—this new eternal life—and you maintain this life by giving heed to what I say. The grace of life, the grace of power, the grace of white-hot unashamed courage comes through my words. Feed the white-hot flame of God's gift with God's Word.

This brings us now to the fourth point in the outline. If the flame of God's gift of courage in suffering is fed by the grace-giving, power-imparting words of Paul, what did he say for the sake of Timothy's fire?

Paul Spoke to Feed the Flame

I see three kinds of things Paul said. I will touch on them only briefly and move from the most intimate to the most eternal.

First, he thanked God for Timothy's authentic faith,
as a father loving his son (2 Tim. 1:3–5).

> *I thank God whom I serve, as did my ancestors [literally: from my parents, 1 Tim 5:4], with a clear conscience, as I remember you constantly in my prayers night and day. As I remember your tears, I long to see you, that I may be filled with joy. I am reminded of your sincere faith, a faith that dwelt first in your grandmother Lois and your mother Eunice and now, I am sure, dwells in you as well.*

Here's my paraphrase—Timothy, I believe with all my heart, that your faith, even though it's rooted in your mother's and your grandmother's faith, is "sincere" (*anupokritou*)—authentic, really yours. You are your own man. You are not mama's boy. You are not gamma's boy. Your faith is yours, even though it was first your mother's and grandmother's.

Don't feel less authentic because of that lineage. My ministry, my service to God, is also "from my parents" (verse 3). I, too, have been deeply shaped by my lineage. Don't begrudge this family influence, Timothy. Glory in it.

My Beloved Child. And if you are wounded or sorrowful or timid because your father was so absent or so passive in your spiritual upbringing, remember—I am your father. I don't call you "my beloved child" (1:2) for sentimental reasons, or merely because God awakened you under my preaching. I call you *my beloved child*, because I am right now being a father to you.

The grace that I am delivering to you right now is coming from your heavenly Father (1:2) and flowing through the words of your spiritual earthly father. That is what I am and love to be. That is why I long to see you, that my joy may be full. I love you. I never had a son. You never had a father with whom you connected spiritually. That is who we are. This is a grace for us, son. Be strong in it (2:1). That's the first thing Paul says to deliver grace and power and courage to Timothy.

Paul gives himself as a pattern of courageous suffering with confidence in God's sustaining grace (2 Tim. 1:11–12).

> *[For the gospel] I was appointed a preacher and apostle and teacher, which is why I suffer as I do. But I am not ashamed, for I know whom I have believed, and I am convinced that he is able to guard until that Day what has been entrusted to me.*

Timothy, when you speak on behalf of the gospel—as preacher or teacher—you will suffer. Consider my life. It has not been easy. But I am not ashamed of the gospel. I am not ashamed of sitting here in prison. And I don't want you to be ashamed either, son.

And the reason we don't have to be ashamed is that the one who entrusted us with the gospel is powerful (*dunatos estin*—he is able; he is powerful, verse 12). He will guard it until we stand before him in judgment. The greatness of his power and the freedom of his grace and his jealousy for the gospel guarantee he will fight for us. He will guard this deposit. He will cause us to feed the white-hot flame of his own gift, until he calls or until he comes. He makes the flame of his gift depend on our feeding and makes our feeding depend on his grace. Don't be ashamed, Timothy. Be courageous for the gospel.

Finally, Paul takes Timothy back into eternity to show that this empowering, sustaining, flame-feeding grace is absolutely free and sovereign and not dependent on anything we do (2 Tim. 1:9–10).

We're ending where we began. Paul does call Timothy to act. *Timothy, keep feeding the white-hot flame of God's gift—of unashamed courage to speak openly of Christ and to suffer for the gospel.* Feed it, Timothy. Do that. Fan that flame. Feed that fire. And every time you preach the Word of grace to yourself and strengthen your heart with blood-bought promises of life and help, look deep into eternity to see why you are doing this. Verses 9–10:

> [He] saved us and called us to a holy calling, not because of our works but because of his own purpose and grace, which he gave us in Christ Jesus before the ages began, and which now has been manifested through the appearing of our Savior Christ Jesus, who abolished death and brought life and immortality to light through the gospel.

Timothy, my son, listen carefully. The grace of God that awakened you and sustains you and strengthens you and feeds the white-hot flame of God's gift in you—that grace was given to you "in Christ Jesus before the ages began."

Before the Ages Began. Timothy, your "name [was] . . . written before the foundation of the world in the book of life of the Lamb who was slain" (Rev. 13:8). Before the creation of the world, God planned creation, the fall, redemption, Christ's coming, and the cross. He planned it all. And he planned you in it.

Why did he do it that way? He did it that way so that you would know beyond the shadow of a doubt your salvation, your calling, your triumph over death, your everlasting life is not because of your works—not your legalistic works and not your works done in righteousness (Titus 3:5), nor anything that you will or feel or think or do.

His Own Purpose and Grace. It is because of "his own purpose and grace" (verse 9). The contrast, Timothy, is not between your works, on one side, and your faith, on the other. The contrast is between your works and your faith and your everything, on one side, and God's purpose and grace before the world ever existed, on the other side.

When Christ died for you, Timothy, to be your punishment and your perfection, and then rose again to abolish death and open everlasting life, what he manifested in that gospel was the eternal purpose of God to be gracious to you. God, for all eternity, has planned to be gracious to you, awaken you, and give you faith, power, unashamed courage, suffering, keeping, and eternal glory.

Keep Feeding the Flame! Therefore, one more time, Timothy, *keep feeding the white-hot flame of God's gift—the unashamed courage to speak openly of Christ and to suffer for the gospel.*

Don't be afraid. I am sure that he will do for you what he has done for me—he will "rescue [you] from every evil deed and bring [you] safely into his heavenly kingdom. To him be the glory forever and ever. Amen" (2 Tim. 4:18).

2

THE PATTERN OF SOUND WORDS

(2 Timothy 1:13–2:13)

Philip Ryken

There are times in life and ministry—many times—when the wind of the Spirit fills a pastor's sails and carries his ministry along by the power of the gospel. I often feel that way after preaching when I see the difference that God's Word makes in people's lives—an angry father vows to stop treating his little girl with foolish rage; a grieving sister leaves her mother's destiny in the hands of her merciful Father in heaven; a sinner comes to saving faith. There may even be times when a pastor's own family is grateful for his ministry. When my oldest son was seven years old he said, "Dad, it is so great that you're our pastor!"

Yet there are also times, many times, when God seems far away and you wonder whether anything you do for Jesus makes a difference. There are times—maybe every week—when you wish that you could preach the same passage again and do it right. There are times when people refuse to follow wise spiritual counsel and instead fall out of "the stupid tree," hitting every branch on the way down. There are times when you face unjust criticism, like the letter that began, "You teach the opposite of what is taught in the Word of God." There are times when the only thing you can do is get on your knees and pray desperately for the help of Jesus.

It is at such times, most of all, that I look ahead to the last of

all days and hope—beyond anything that I could *ever* deserve—
that I will hear my Savior say, "Well done, good and faithful
servant. . . . Enter into the joy of your master" (Matt. 25:21).
Everything I do in ministry is motivated by this ambition—to
be faithful through suffering in the calling that Jesus gave me to
serve as a minister of his gospel. Where will I stand on the Great
Day? Will I fulfill my sacred trust?

The apostle Paul had the same concern for Timothy. As he
wrote to his young brother in gospel ministry, he called him to be
faithful. The section of 2 Timothy that runs from 1:13 to 2:13 is
unified by the apostle's concern for faithfulness in Christian life
and ministry, with all its suffering.

AN APOSTOLIC CALL TO FAITHFUL MINISTRY

First, Paul gives Timothy *an apostolic call to faithful ministry*.
Having reminded Timothy of how he came to faith and having
exhorted him to holy boldness in using his spiritual gift, Paul said
to him, "Follow the pattern of the sound words that you have
heard from me, in the faith and love that are in Christ Jesus. By
the Holy Spirit who dwells within us, guard the good deposit
entrusted to you" (2 Tim. 1:13–14).

This call to faithful ministry is at the same time both doctrinal and practical. When Paul tells Timothy to follow a pattern,
he is reminding the young man that he has been given a model
for ministry. The word "pattern" is said to denote "an outline
sketch or ground-plan used by an artist, or, in literature, a rough
draft forming the basis for a fuller exposition."[1] It does not contain all the details, therefore, but it does define the contours of
a faithful ministry.

This pattern is made up of "words"—of things that Paul

---

[1]J. N. D. Kelly, *The Pastoral Epistles: 1 Timothy, 2 Timothy, Titus*, Harper's New Testament
Commentaries (San Francisco: Harper & Row, 1960), 166.

has said. What the apostle seems mainly to have in mind are the words he used to preach the gospel. Paul is talking about the apostolic message of the person and work of Christ—the propositional truths of his authentic deity and perfect humanity, of his cross and his empty tomb. The content of these words is further clarified at the end of verse 14, where Paul tells Timothy, "guard the good deposit entrusted to you."

The apostle had used identical language at the end of his first letter to Timothy (see 1 Tim. 6:20). Here he reminds his protégé that he has been given a sacred trust. Paul was constantly concerned that false teaching would come in and destroy the church. So he exhorted Timothy to keep the sacred trust of sound doctrine, not to distort the message that he had been given, but to keep it, protect it, and guard it for the church.

A faithful minister keeps the faith. This is essential both to his own spiritual health and to the vitality of the people he serves. When Paul says that these words are "sound," he means that they are wholesome, nurturing, and health-producing. Some people say that doctrine kills, but this way of thinking is completely alien to the apostle, who believed that sound doctrine brings life and health to the people of God.

But this is true, of course, only when that doctrine is not merely a theological speculation but a practical way of life. Paul described sound doctrine as something to follow "in the faith and love that are in Christ Jesus" (2 Tim. 1:13). John Calvin agreed, and was right when he said that saving faith is not an "empty speculation" that merely "flits about in the top of the brain," but something that "takes root in the depth of the heart."[2]

The call to faithful ministry is not simply to accept a particular set of beliefs or to carry out a certain job description; it is a

---

[2]John Calvin, *Institutes of the Christian Religion*, ed. John T. McNeill, trans. Ford Lewis Battles; 2 vols. (Library of Christian Classics; Philadelphia: Westminster, 1960), 3.2.36.

way of life that is shaped by the gospel of Jesus Christ. It is a life of faith in which I am called to trust God for everything—the gifts I need for ministry, the insight I need into the Word, the wisdom I need for spiritual counsel, the vision I need for the future, whatever resources I need to do what God has called me to do. To be faithful to the call is to trust Jesus for *everything*.

The gospel way of life is also a life of love, in which I am called to give myself away for Jesus. I remember talking with one of my elders about accepting another term of service. He was hesitant because of all the responsibilities he had—to provide for his wife and children, to care for his employees, to fulfill his personal ministry in the lives of other people. I detected just the hint of a complaint when he said, "Soon I won't have any time left for me." I said, "Well, that's really living, isn't it, when Jesus teaches you how to live completely for others?"

This is the call that God has placed on every believer's life and ministry. It is a doctrinal and practical call, united with Christ and empowered by the Holy Spirit. It is a call to trust in Jesus and love other people.

Be clear about God's definition for success in ministry. It has little or nothing to do with the size of someone's ministry or with having more political influence or being hip or trendy or traditional or non-traditional or being whatever kind of church happens to appeal to you. A successful ministry is simply this— a faithful ministry, faithful to Jesus Christ in life and doctrine, and faithful in safe-keeping and living out his idol-destroying gospel.

A PERSONAL EXAMPLE OF FAITHFUL MINISTRY

The sad reality is that although some people answer this call, many people do not. We are reminded of this in verses 15 to 18, in which Paul gives Timothy *an example of faithful ministry* (and also, as it happens, some examples of people who fell away from faithful ministry altogether).

The bad examples come first, "You are aware that all who are in Asia turned away from me, among whom are Phygelus and Hermogenes" (2 Tim. 1:15). Paul is not complaining here or feeling sorry for himself because he feels all alone. He is simply giving us the facts—everyone has abandoned him.

It seems almost certain that Paul was in prison at the time; possibly this was during the deadly persecutions of Nero. So perhaps it is not surprising that most Christians, for fear of their own torment, had distanced themselves from Paul and his ministry. Still, the extent of their apostasy is distressing. In chapter 4 we will learn that only Luke is still by the apostle's side (2 Tim. 4:11). Demas has deserted him completely because of his love for the present world (2 Tim. 4:10). Alexander has not just abandoned Paul, he attacked him (2 Tim. 4:14). No one stood by him. His former helpers have not been faithful to the call of Christ.

Among the deserters and defectors were Phygelus and Hermogenes. But these men are not the only apostates, of course. Many people have abandoned the ministry. It happens all the time—every day, in fact. Seventeen hundred ministers leave the ministry every month. Half of the people who are still in the ministry have considered leaving the ministry in the last few months, and only half of those who are starting out will last five years. Barely one in ten will actually retire as a minister. It is not hard to understand why. Indeed, it is hard to blame them. Ninety percent of pastors work fifty-five to seventy-five hours a week. Eighty percent believe that pastoral ministry has negatively affected their families. At least half feel unable to meet the high demands of the job, maybe because ninety percent of them feel inadequately trained.[3]

These are just statistics, of course, but anyone who has been in ministry for long knows some of the stories behind them— pastors caught in sexual sin, men who have left the ministry for a homosexual partner, friends who grew weary of serving God in a struggling situation and took a nine-to-five job instead, maybe even someone who left the faith completely.

This is not to say that pastoral ministry is the only good way to serve God, or even the best way to serve God. Nor is it to say that everyone who is in pastoral ministry ought to stay in pastoral ministry. But it is hard to be faithful in this calling. Falling away is at least as common now as it was then. So when we hear Paul tell Timothy this cautionary tale, we need to admit that there is a real possibility that we ourselves could end up as failures in ministry. Indeed, apart from the indwelling Spirit that Paul mentioned in verse 14, we would certainly fall away. But by the grace of God, we may remain faithful to the call.

Here we can take encouragement from the other example that Paul gives—an example of faithfulness in ministry. Here is what Paul said about his friend Onesiphorus:

> May the Lord grant mercy to the household of Onesiphorus, for he often refreshed me and was not ashamed of my chains, but when he arrived in Rome he searched for me earnestly and found me—may the Lord grant him to find mercy from the Lord on that Day!— and you well know all the service he rendered at Ephesus. (2 Tim. 1:16–18)

Paul introduces Onesiphorus as an outstanding example of faithful ministry. The virtues of this godly man are characteristics of every faithful ministry.

[3]Pastoral Care Inc. http://pastoralcareinc.com/WhyPastoralCare/Statistics.html.

Onesiphorus loved the men who preached God's Word and sought to encourage them in ministry. Paul tells us that Onesiphorus often refreshed him. Possibly this means that he provided for Paul's practical needs in prison. Very likely it also means that he blessed Paul with the spiritual gift of his friendship; Onesiphorus was a blessing to the apostle's soul.

This is a good test for anyone—Do I love the men that God has put in ministry? To be more pointed—Do I see some of my fellow ministers as rivals, wishing that I had the situation or the reputation that they have? Do I feel a little tinge of regret when someone else is elevated, or conversely, a little surge of pleasure when someone has the kind of trouble that I secretly think he deserves? Or am I able instead to rejoice in the success that God has given to others because my primary commitment is to the gospel? The example of Onesiphorus encourages us to be explicit and intentional in our efforts to support the preaching of God's Word and the people who preach it.

The love that Onesiphorus had for gospel ministry was equaled by his courage. When this brother went to Rome, he was taking his life into his own hands. The church was under persecution, which explains why it was hard for him to find the apostle Paul. If people knew where Paul was, they weren't saying. No one wanted to get in trouble with Nero. But Onesiphorus was not concerned with his own safety if there was kingdom work to be done. He was willing to suffer hardship, and he was not ashamed to be associated with a man who was an enemy of the state as long as that man, too, was faithful to the gospel.

Ministry takes courage—sometimes unusual courage. It takes courage to expose idolatry or to cross ethnic and social lines with the gospel. It takes courage to stand up and say that Jesus is the only way, not just for Christians, but also for Muslims and atheists. It takes courage to go to the hard places in the world and share the gospel. But this is what faithfulness requires.

We can also say this about Onesiphorus—he was fruitful wherever he went. He was effective not only in Rome, but also in Ephesus. Paul ends the chapter by saying, "You well know all the service he rendered at Ephesus" (2 Tim. 1:18). People who are faithful in ministry are useful wherever they go. Many ministers move from one place to another over the course of a lifetime in ministry (and not always to places they would choose to go). But whatever the situation, a faithful minister is always fruitful. Everything we see in Onesiphorus is characteristic of a faithful minister. He supports the work of other preachers. He is unashamed of the gospel, especially when it is under attack, and thus he is fruitful wherever he goes.

Such a ministry is under the mercy of God. Here Paul prays that Onesiphorus may "find mercy from the Lord on that Day!"—meaning the day of judgment (2 Tim. 1:18). Paul was looking beyond the present hardships of ministry to the last of all days, when faithful ministers will receive their merciful reward. His prayer for Onesiphorus was not an idle wish. Nor is it a plea for him to be accepted on his own merits. Rather, it is a God-honoring prayer that God will surely answer—to accept Onesiphorus (and everyone who follows his example) by the mercy of Jesus and say to him, "Well done, good and faithful servant; enter into the joy of your master."

A SACRED TRUST TRANSMITTED TO FAITHFUL MEN

Paul has given Timothy a call to faithful ministry with a faithful example to follow. In chapter 2 the apostle gives Timothy further instructions about his sacred trust. He begins by charging him to perpetuate the faith—*what might well be termed a sacred trust transmitted to faithful men.* Paul writes, "You then, my child, be strengthened by the grace that is in Christ Jesus, and what you have heard from me in the presence of many witnesses entrust to faithful men who will be able to teach others also" (2 Tim. 2:1–2).

Much more could be said about Paul's marvelous exhortation here to "be strengthened by the grace that is in Christ Jesus" (2 Tim. 2:1). It is characteristic of the apostle to see the hard work of gospel ministry empowered by the grace of God. To the Corinthians he said, "By the grace of God I am what I am, and his grace toward me was not in vain. On the contrary, I worked harder than any of them, though it was not I, but the grace of God that is with me" (1 Cor. 15:10).

This is the secret to persevering through long years in the pastorate or of surviving a season of ministry that seems like a crucifixion. Yes, we are called to work hard, and Paul will say more about this in a moment. But Jesus himself is our strength. His grace is sufficient for us—his unmerited favor for people like us, who do not even deserve to be in the ministry. Nevertheless, we are carried along by his mighty power. Our strength is in his grace.

When I am worn down by the cares of life and ministry, and wonder if I have anything left to give, I often reflect on Colossians 1:29. Dick Lucas, who preached for many years at St. Helen's Bishopsgate in London, once told me that this verse was a mainstay for him in ministry; so I wrote it down on a little slip of paper and taped it to my computer. The apostle Paul had been talking about his preaching, how he labored to give people Christ and warn them away from sin, striving for their sanctification. Then he said, "For this I toil, struggling with all his energy that he powerfully works within me" (Col. 1:29). When we have the grace that is in Jesus, we do not work in our own natural strength, but by the power of Almighty God.

But we digress. Paul's burden in these verses is for Timothy to teach others what he has learned for himself. A transmission must take place in which the same apostolic gospel that Paul gave to Timothy is handed on to the following generation. There is some debate about what he means by "many witnesses," but Paul seems to be talking about something like public ordination, in which a minister is set apart for gospel work in the public worship of the church.

As an ordained minister, Timothy had received something from Paul—the sound pattern and the good deposit that were mentioned back in chapter 1. Now he has a responsibility to pass the same core doctrines of the Christian faith along to others. Paul is looking for a few faithful men—or maybe more than a few.

We should have the same burden for the rising generation in our own day. We know that the church of Jesus Christ will endure as long as time shall last. But we also know that in any particular culture, the church is never more than one generation away from extinction. Thus, one of our primary and perpetual responsibilities in propagating the faith is to pass our ministry on to faithful men.

I remember my own mentors in ministry—fathers in the faith—faithful men who entrusted the gospel to me, so that now my ministry is part of the fulfillment of their calling. Some of these men were elders in the church, including my father and grandfathers: Frank Ryken, Albert Graham, Leland Ryken—men of quiet conviction and genuine faith. Others were my pastors, like my pastor while I was growing up, Bob Harvey, who had a special gift for connecting the Old and New Testaments. Others are men I served for a time, but have now gone on to their eternal reward: William Still from Scotland and James Montgomery Boice. And there are so many others. If it takes a village to raise a child, it also takes a whole church to raise a minister.

Now, increasingly, I see my own pastorate as one of transmission and not just reception. Even if I am not yet anyone's "father in the faith," I have a responsibility to my younger brothers. Yesterday, I was just starting out in ministry. Tomorrow, I will finish my race. As I work today—trying in ministry, and sometimes failing, but always wanting to be faithful—I pass a sacred trust along to others.

My friend Randall Grossman serves as the pastor of a middle-sized church in Pennsylvania. He has the holy ambition that God would allow him to train twenty pastors by the time he retires from the ministry. His example challenges me to ask a question that every pastor should ask—What sacred trust have I received, and how am I preparing to pass it along to others?

When we look at the history of the church, we see an unbroken chain of gospel ministry—an evangelical succession. To give just one example, in the early seventeenth century the Cambridge preacher Richard Sibbes wrote a book about the comforting work of Christ called *The Bruised Reed*. One of the people who read that book was a tinker, who gave a copy to a boy named Richard Baxter, who became one of the greatest preachers in the Puritan church. Baxter wrote *A Call to the Unconverted*, which made a dramatic difference in the life of Philip Doddridge—this was in the early eighteenth century. Doddridge, in turn, wrote a book called *The Rise and Progress of Religion in the Soul*, which was a means of saving and sanctifying grace in the life of William Wilberforce, who was the primary human instrument in the abolition of the slave trade. The influence continues, because

Wilberforce is still seen as a heroic example in the fight against evil in our own day.[4]

One of the most important ways we keep the faith is by passing on the faith. Take what you have heard and entrust it to faithful men, who in turn will be able to preach it to many others.

OCCUPATIONAL ILLUSTRATIONS OF FAITHFUL WORK

Like any good preacher, the apostle Paul often illustrated gospel truth with examples from daily life. In 2 Timothy 2:3–7 he gives three *occupational illustrations of faithful work*. I call them "occupational" because in them Paul mentions three of the hardest-working jobs that anyone can do. In doing so, the apostle highlights three different aspects of faithfulness: its focus, its diligence, and its reward.

Soldier

Paul's first illustration comes from the military: "Share in suffering as a good soldier of Christ Jesus. No soldier gets entangled in civilian pursuits, since his aim is to please the one who enlisted him" (2 Tim. 2:3–4).

The comparison here is multifaceted. Serving in the army involves a lot of suffering, especially in wartime, which is why recruiters call it "the toughest job you'll ever love." Soldiers suffer the trials of basic training, the loss of personal freedom, the fatigue of combat. All of this makes military service an apt metaphor for pastoral ministry, which engages us in spiritual warfare. To serve in ministry is to share in the sufferings of Christ. No one knew this any better than the apostle Paul, who had made it his ambition to share in the sufferings of his Savior (see Phil. 3:10–11).

Ministry is also like the military in another respect—it

---

[4]Kent Hughes, *1 and 2 Timothy and Titus*, Preaching the Word (Wheaton: Crossway, 2000), 193–94.

requires a total life commitment that is kept free from daily distractions. In mentioning "civilian pursuits," Paul may have been thinking of something like the Roman military code, which stated, "We forbid men engaged in military service to engage in civilian occupations."[5] If he values his life, a soldier at war does not have time to worry about anything else except doing his daily duty.

Do not misunderstand this verse—it does not rule out bi-vocational ministry when necessary. Nor does it give pastors license to neglect their families. Elisabeth Elliot used to say that when he was in college, Jim Elliot, the famous missionary and Christian martyr, gave her 2 Timothy 2:4 to explain why he could not get involved in a romantic relationship (not exactly the way to a woman's heart!). Never forget that the first calling of any married man is to his wife and children. Never use pastoral position as an excuse for neglecting family life.

Yet the point of this verse still stands—do not get distracted from the ministry that God has called you to do. Don't waste time. If you need to prepare a sermon, don't spend thirty minutes reading the news and visiting a theological blog site. Don't do all the easy things before you get around to the hard things, but do the thing that most needs to be done. If there is a phone call that you would rather not make, to a person that you would rather not deal with, make that call first. If there is a hard conversation that needs to take place, do not keep hoping that the situation will get better on its own, but set up a time to address the issue, asking for the help of the Holy Spirit. Limit the time you spend on entertainment, hobbies, and other outside interests to the amount of time that is appropriate for someone who is living in spiritual wartime, not kingdom peacetime. J. N. D. Kelly sum-

---

[5]Hughes, *1 and 2 Timothy and Titus*, 195.

marizes by saying that Christian leaders "should cut out of their lives anything, however good in itself, which is liable to deflect them from total service to Christ."[6]

The motivation for such single-minded ministry comes at the end of verse 4—a soldier wants to please his commanding officer. We are called to serve the Lord Jesus Christ, who is the warrior of our salvation and our great Captain in the spiritual fight. As we go about our ministry in the church, and everything else we do in life, we should ask ourselves questions like these: Is this something that will please my Commanding Officer? Am I doing this the way that he wants me to do it? Pastoral ministry is not just a job; it is a calling for which am I accountable. The goal of that calling is well expressed in the motto of the United States Marines: *Semper fidelis!* Always faithful!

Athlete

The second occupational illustration comes from the world of sports: "An athlete is not crowned unless he competes according to the rules" (2 Tim. 2:5). Here the apostle uses another demanding calling to highlight another kind of faithfulness—playing by the rules. He may have in mind the rules of the game itself, like the *Official Rules of Major League Baseball* for example. But it is often thought that Paul is referring instead to the regulations that governed the training regimen for athletes competing in the ancient Isthmian or Olympic games. In order to maintain high standards of competition, athletes typically began their workouts, which could last for as long as ten months, by taking an oath that they would train according to the rules, or else be disqualified.[7]

---

[6]Kelly, *Pastoral Epistles*, 175.
[7]Philip H. Towner, *1–2 Timothy and Titus*, IVP New Testament Commentary (Downers Grove, IL: InterVarsity, 1994), 173.

How does this illustration apply to gospel ministry? Possibly as a reminder to play by the righteous rules of the Christian life, rather than giving in to envy, greed, hypocrisy, and all the other forms of immorality that are especially tempting to ministers. But maybe it would be better to take this verse as an exhortation to work hard in ministry—as hard as an Olympian. Work hard to understand and apply the Word of God, both in your own life and for the people you serve. Work hard in the spiritual labor of prayer. Work hard at discipleship, training, and evangelism. The Puritan William Perkins had a memorable phrase he used to remind him of his duty. "You are a minister of the gospel," he would say to himself, and then he would quote the Latin epigram *hoc age*, which means, "Do this!" (loosely paraphrased, "Get with it!").

When we approach ministry with this kind of work ethic, we remain eligible for the crowning prize. Paul often uses the image of an athlete crowned with victory—not as a reward of merit, of course, but as a gift of grace for faithful champions. This is part of our motivation for ministry. We are looking for the crown of glory that will follow the cross of suffering.

The Puritan Richard Sibbes took the same perspective when he advised his fellow pastors to wait for the rewards of their ministry:[8]

> Let us commit the fame and credit, of what we are or do to God. He will take care of that, let us take care to be and to do as we should, and then for noise and report, let it be good or ill as God will send it. . . . Therefore let us labour to be good in secret. . . . We should be carried with the Spirit of God, and with a holy desire to serve God and our brethren, and to do all the good we can, and never care for the speeches of the world.

---

[8]Richard Sibbes, *Works of Richard Sibbes*, ed. Alexander Grant (1862–64; repr., Edinburgh: Banner of Truth, 1973), 1:23–24.

Then Sibbes closed with this comment, "We'll have glory enough BY-AND-BY."

Farmer

Next the apostle turns from athletics to agriculture. His third illustration comes from down on the farm: "It is the hardworking farmer who ought to have the first share of the crops. Think over what I say, for the Lord will give you understanding in everything" (2 Tim. 2:6–7). Once again, Paul chooses a hardworking occupation as illustration for faithfulness. In fact, the farmer may be the hardest worker of all—up before dawn, working all day, exhausted by nightfall—just like pastoral ministry! J. N. D. Kelly makes the provocative comment that the word Paul uses here for work (*kopiōnta*) is virtually a synonym for pastoral ministry.[9]

Here again faithfulness has its reward. Paul mentions "the first share of the crops," which many take as a way of indicating that ministers have a right to receive remuneration, especially since Paul uses similar metaphors in some of his other letters (see 1 Cor. 9:9–10; 1 Tim. 5:17–18). But these metaphors of faithfulness also have a wider application. The most important harvest for a hard-working pastor is the one that he reaps for sowing the good seed of God's Word—the harvest of the gospel.

All three of the occupations that Paul mentions require faithful hard work and dedicated, undistracted labor. All of them entail hardship and suffering. But they also hold the promise of a reward. "Beyond warfare is victory, beyond the athlete's effort is the prize, and beyond agricultural labor is the crop."[10] So work faithfully for the gospel reward, which God will bring in his own good time.

[9]Kelly, *Pastoral Epistles*, 176.
[10]C. K. Barrett, *The Pastoral Epistles* (Oxford: Oxford University Press, 1963), 102.

God's reward for faithful ministry is beautifully illustrated by the story of Luke Short, converted at the tender age of 103. Mr. Short was sitting under a hedge in Virginia when he happened to remember a sermon he had once heard preached by the famous Puritan John Flavel. As he recalled the sermon, he asked God to forgive his sins right then and there, through the death and resurrection of Jesus Christ. Short lived for three more years, and when he died, the following words were inscribed on his tombstone, "Here lies a babe in grace, aged three years, who died according to nature, aged 106."

Here is the truly remarkable part of the story. The sermon that old Mr. Short remembered had been preached *eighty-five* years earlier back in England! Nearly a century passed between Flavel's sermon and Short's conversion, between the sowing and the reaping.[11] Sooner or later, by the grace of God, faithful work always has its reward.

A COMMAND TO REMEMBER THE FAITHFUL SAVIOR

It is good to hear the apostolic exhortations to faithful ministry. However, we need to make sure that we do not get the impression that ministry is more a matter of law than of grace, that it mainly depends on our effort rather than God's empowerment.

No one is more careful to avoid this error than the apostle Paul, as we see throughout 2 Timothy 1:13–2:13. Again and again, Paul grounds ministry in the gospel. Paul's call to faithful ministry in chapter 1 is to a ministry in Christ Jesus and by the Holy Spirit (2 Tim. 1:13–14). His example of faithful ministry in verses 16 to 18 is a man who is under the mercy of God. The commands in chapter 2, including the illustrations of hard work,

---

[11]See John Flavel, *The Mystery of Providence* (Edinburgh: Banner of Truth, 1963), 11.

are all strengthened by the grace of Jesus (verse 1) and instructed by the wisdom of Jesus (verse 7).

Yet the gospel is made even more explicit in verses 8 through 10, where the apostle gives us *a gospel command to remember a faithful Savior*. As this part of the epistle builds to its Christ-centered climax, Paul says, "Remember Jesus Christ, risen from the dead, the offspring of David, as preached in my gospel, for which I am suffering, bound with chains as a criminal. But the word of God is not bound!" (2 Tim. 2:8–9).

Every faithful ministry is founded on the faithful Savior. As we follow the example of faithful men like Onesiphorus, striving to work hard in the strength of the grace of God, we are commanded to remember Jesus Christ, not simply as a mental exercise, but as a lifelong commitment to live for him.

From the beginning of this letter, Paul has been reminding Timothy of many things that he should remember: his forefathers in the faith (2 Tim. 1:3), his friendship with Paul (2 Tim. 1:4), the faith that lived in his family's heart (2 Tim. 1:5), and the flame of his spiritual gifts (2 Tim. 1:6–7). Now he tells Timothy to remember the most important thing of all—the gospel itself.

Jesus Christ is "risen from the dead," Paul says (2 Tim. 2:8). This calls to mind the crucifixion, when Jesus died for sinners, and even more so the resurrection, when Jesus came up from the grave with the power of eternal life. This is the same gospel that Paul always preached, the gospel of the cross and the empty tomb (cf. 1 Cor. 15:3–4). We are called to remember the faithful, saving work of Jesus as the life-giving source of our salvation.

We should also remember who Jesus is. He is "the offspring of David" (2 Tim. 2:8). This title testifies to the true humanity of Jesus Christ, that he was and is truly a man. It also testifies to his royal majesty. Jesus came from the royal line of David, and thus he is the rightful heir to the noblest of all kingly thrones, the throne of the house of Judah.

This is the gospel Paul preached, and for which he suffered. In verse 9 he tells us that he was chained like a common "criminal" (*kakourgos*), a term typically reserved for thieves, traitors, and murderers (e.g., Luke 23:32). Yet the Word of God is not bound! Despite all of Satan's best efforts to shut out the gospel by locking down the servants of God, the Word still does its work in the world. As the great preacher John Chrysostom once said on this text, "For just as it is not possible to bind a sunbeam, so neither the preaching of the word; and what was much more, the teacher was bound, and yet the word flew abroad; he inhabited the prison, and yet his doctrine rapidly winged its way every where throughout the world!"[12]

This is why it is such a tragedy when people think that there is something apart from or something in addition to the Word of God that will accomplish the spiritual work of the church. The Word works. Indeed, it is the only thing that *does* work. What teaches us the truth about God? What convinces us that we are sinners who need a Savior? What offers us Jesus for the forgiveness of our sins? What teaches us the way to worship, the way to live, and the way to serve? What makes preaching and evangelism and discipleship effective? It is the Word that the Holy Spirit has unbound and unchained for the salvation and the sanctification of the people of God.

Many stories can be told about the freedom of God's Word to do its work. Here is just one, from Stavropol, Russia, where in the 1930s Joseph Stalin ordered every Bible in the city to be confiscated. After the fall of communism, the agency CoMission

---

[12]John Chrysostom, *Concerning the Statues—Homily XVI*, quoted in Thomas C. Oden, *First and Second Timothy and Titus* (Louisville, KY: Westminster, 1989), 50.

sent a team to Stavropol. When they were having difficulty getting enough Bibles shipped from Moscow, one of the locals mentioned the warehouse outside of town where he had heard that Bibles were stored since the days of Stalin. So the team borrowed a truck, recruited a couple of workers, and went to unload the Bibles.

One of the men they hired was hostile to the Christian faith, a college skeptic who was there only for the money. After working for a little while, the man slipped off by himself. When they found him later, sitting in a corner, he was weeping over a copy of the Scriptures. The skeptic had picked up a Bible, and when he opened it he saw that it was signed by his own grandmother, who had long prayed for his salvation![13] God's Word cannot be bound; it always does its work in the world, even in the hearts and minds of people who think they do not even want to believe it.

When we have such a powerful Word to share, a Word that proclaims the grace of your faithful Savior, we can endure any and every hardship to preach it, as Paul did. Remembering Jesus reminded the apostle why he was in the ministry. "Therefore I endure everything," he said, "for the sake of the elect, that they also may obtain the salvation that is in Christ Jesus with eternal glory" (2 Tim. 2:10).

We endure the suffering of ministry for the sake of the glory—not our own glory, but the glory that Jesus has promised to share with his people. When Paul speaks here about "the elect," he is thinking primarily of people who have not yet come to faith in Jesus Christ, but are still predestined for salvation. It is for those chosen ones that we remember the gospel of Jesus and preach his Word. It is for the people in our families who

---

[13]Andrea Wolfe, "An Answered Prayer from Stalin's Times," *The Chariot* 2, no. 1:1.

have not yet come to Christ; for neighbors who say they want to come to church sometime, but never do; for people who are lost in the city, whether they are lost in poverty or greed. It is for the forgotten children of a suffering world; it is for the tens of millions who will sleep tonight and wake up tomorrow morning without ever having heard that the Son of God came to die for their sins and then rise with new life for the world. It is for their sakes that we remember Jesus well enough to remain faithful in ministry.

THE ABSOLUTE FAITHFULNESS OF A FAITHFUL GOD

This brings us at last to one of the most beautiful passages in the entire Bible. Here is one of Paul's "trustworthy sayings," which may have been part of an early Christian hymn, perhaps used at the time of baptism:

> *If we have died with him, we will also live with him;*
> *if we endure, we will also reign with him;*
> *if we deny him, he also will deny us;*
> *if we are faithless, he remains faithful—*
>
> *for he cannot deny himself (2 Tim. 2:11–13).*

This is holy ground, for here the Scripture bears witness to the absolute faithfulness of a faithful God and gives his promise of grace to people who sometimes fail in ministry.

Follow the logic of these verses all the way to their surprising conclusion. Paul begins by taking the faithful Savior that he preached in verses 8 through 10 and uniting us to him for our salvation. Jesus died; Jesus rose again; Jesus ascended to glory. And when Jesus did these things, he did them for our salvation. So when Jesus died on the cross, we died with him; our sins were put to death in the death of Christ. When Jesus rose from the grave, we rose with him; we have received the eternal life that he brought with him up out of the empty tomb.

Now, if we endure, if we persevere through suffering in the Christian faith, if we remain faithful in ministry, then we, too, will come into a kingdom. We will reign with Jesus Christ. Here the apostle is simply proclaiming our union with Christ as it relates to our endurance in ministry. By faith we are joined to Jesus in everything he did for our salvation: death, resurrection, and ascension (cf. Rom. 6:4–5).

But will we remain faithful? That is the question. Verse 12 begins with a condition, "if we endure." But will we endure? Paul's urgent concern throughout this entire section of 2 Timothy has been faithfulness in ministry. He has called us to be faithful to the gospel, but he also warned us that not everyone remains faithful to that call, especially when that call is so demanding, like serving in the military or training for the Olympics or working a farm.

Sadly, some people, including some pastors, end up denying Jesus Christ. Sadder still, as a consequence of their apostasy, they themselves will be denied at the final judgment. "If we deny him, he also will deny us." Jesus said it himself, "Whoever denies me before men, I also will deny before my Father who is in heaven" (Matt. 10:33). What we do with Jesus is a matter of eternal life and death.

Then Paul adds another category, which seems to stand as a parallel, "If we are faithless. . . ." But here there is an unexpected turn of phrase, a gospel twist that opens up such wide mysteries in the love of God that it is possible for people like us to be accepted by God. "If we are faithless," what then? We will be rejected? We will be disqualified? We will be condemned? No!

"If we are faithless, he remains faithful—for he cannot deny himself" (2 Tim. 2:13).

Understand that when Paul talks about being "faithless," he is not talking about a final, irrevocable, and fatal rejection of Jesus Christ. He is talking about all the times that we fail in life and ministry, the times that we fail to trust God or obey God or serve God the way we know we should—the half-baked sermon, the unprayed prayer, the self-defensive response that put somebody else down. He is talking about all the times we wimp out in ministry because we are not white-hot with the gospel.

Nevertheless, God is still faithful. How could he be anything but faithful? It is God's very nature to be consistent with himself and with all the promises he made before the world began. He would have to un-God himself to be unfaithful.

ROLL CALL OF THE FAITHFUL

Understand what this means for ministry—even our unfaithfulness cannot stop the gospel work that God will do, including all the work that he still wants to do through us.

Many faithless men could testify to the truth of this great claim, men who in some way failed in life and ministry, yet still offered useful service to the kingdom of God because of the faithfulness of Jesus Christ.

Think, for example, of Adam. The father of us all could say, "Brothers, I was faithless in my calling as a husband and father. When Eve ate the forbidden fruit, I should have offered my life to God as the atonement for her sin, but I chose the idol of reason. I wanted to know what she knew, and so I sinned to the ruin of us all. But God is still faithful. He kept his promise to provide a Savior to crush Satan under his feet and to bring many of my sons and daughters to glory. So I tell you it is true—if we are faithless, he remains faithful, for he cannot deny himself."

Consider Abraham, our father in the faith. Here is the testimony that he could give: "Brothers, I was faithless in life and ministry. Idolizing control, I doubted the promises of God and tried to come up with my own way of fulfilling God's promise. In doing so, I sowed seeds of discord that divide the human race today. But God is still faithful. He has given me children of faith as countless as the stars in the evening sky. I tell you, even if we are faithless, he remains faithful."

Or think of David, the royal king, and the testimony that he could give. "Brothers, I was faithless to do my duty. To my own shame, I must confess that I was a murderer and an adulterer—idolatries of power and sex. But God is still faithful. He blotted out my transgressions, he cleansed me from all my sin, and he kept his promise to put my son on the everlasting throne. So I say, even if we are faithless, he remains faithful."

Think even of Peter. Peter? Yes, because rather than casting doubt on the truth of 2 Timothy 2, that denying disciple is the best proof of its doctrine. Peter could say, "Brothers, and sisters, I too was faithless in life and ministry. On the night that Jesus was betrayed, I denied him three different ways before breakfast. But God is still faithful. My faithful Savior prayed that my faith would not fail. So my fall was only temporary; it was not a full or fatal denial. And after he rose from the dead, Jesus did what he said and called me back into ministry. I tell you, even if we are faithless, he remains faithful."

Yet the best proof of the absolute faithfulness of God is not the testimony of mortal men; the best proof is the cross of Jesus Christ.

Understand what the Son of God had to do in order to make

good on this promise, that God remains faithful. The penalty for unfaithfulness to God is death. This is something that Adam and Abraham both knew. Adam understood it because God said to him, "In the day that you eat of it you shall surely die" (Gen 2:17). Abraham understood it because when God made a covenant with him, dividing the sacrificial animals in two, God himself passed through the pieces (see Genesis 15), which was a way of promising that he would take responsibility for both sides of the covenant—not just his side of the bargain, but also Abraham's. So if Abraham proved faithless, then God himself would suffer the punishment for Abraham's sin, or else be unfaithful to his promise.

Therefore, remaining faithful meant death and the cross. When Jesus saw our lost condition, he knew what it would take to redeem us. It would cost him his very life, for he knew, as the Scripture says, it was necessary for the Christ to suffer these things before he entered into his glory (Luke 24:26). But Jesus was committed to do it. "Although they are faithless," he said to the Father, "I will remain faithful, for I cannot deny myself. I cannot deny the promises that I have made—the promise to destroy the devil, the promise to bless all nations, the promise of a forever kingdom. I will therefore suffer and die for my people's sins."

When Jesus hung naked and bleeding on the cross, it was for the sins of Adam and Abraham and David and Peter and everyone else in the family of God. It was for lying and theft and adultery and murder and all the rest of our faithless sins, including all the sins we commit in ministry. Even to the death, Jesus did not fail, but paid for all our sins.

The Father did not fail either. He kept the promise of his Word, "I will not . . . be false to my faithfulness" (Ps. 89:33). So when Jesus offered a perfect sacrifice for sin, the Father accepted that sacrifice. When he saw the Son suffering and dying for sin, he said, "Well done, good and faithful Servant." Then, as the proof of his approval, on the third day he raised him from the dead. The Father did this because he cannot deny himself. Having promised salvation, he followed through on the resurrection. This is the absolute faithfulness of God.

Now we are accepted by that grace. In explaining the present ministry of Jesus Christ as our great High Priest, the *Westminster Larger Catechism* says that right now Jesus stands before his Father's throne, in his crucified and risen body, to defend us against the judgment of God. Jesus tells the Father to take the merits of his perfect obedience and his substitutionary atonement and apply them to us. Jesus does this in spite of the fact—indeed, he does it *because* of the fact—that we are faithless in life and ministry every day. And when Jesus does this, the *Catechism* says, he procures for us the acceptance of "our persons *and our services.*"

It is not just our persons that are accepted by God because of the faithfulness of Jesus Christ, but also our services, that is, all the things we do for God in ministry. We are called to be faithful in the sacred trust of gospel ministry. But the acceptance of our ministry does not depend on our faithfulness to God, but on his faithfulness to his Word. Admittedly, our ministry isn't what it could be. At times we may wonder whether anything we have ever done for Jesus is worth anything at all. Or perhaps, after failing, we doubt whether God can still use us. It is at such times, most of all, that we need to remember Jesus Christ and know that we are loved and accepted by God. Even our own ministry is accepted on the basis of his perfect life, atoning death, and glorious resurrection.

Even if we are not really sure if we could ever be any kind of success in ministry, we should still try for Jesus, and when we fail for Jesus, we should believe this promise, "If we are faithless, he remains faithful—for he cannot deny himself."

3

THE MARKS OF POSITIVE MINISTRY

(2 Timothy 2:14–26)

Mark Driscoll

Saul was so violently opposed to Jesus Christ that he zealously persecuted and murdered Christians. But Jesus returned from heaven to convert Saul, who then adopted the Christian name Paul and became a pastor and missionary. His courageous travels brought the gospel to many people who had never heard of Jesus, including a town called Lystra where a young man named Timothy lived (Acts 14:8–20). Though Paul was beaten, dragged outside of the city, and left for dead, the truth of Jesus apparently converted the young Timothy, who later joined Paul's ministry (Acts 16:1–4).

Paul loved young Timothy, affectionately referring to him as a son (Phil. 2:22; 1 Tim. 1:2; 2 Tim. 1:2). These men are virtually inseparable throughout the New Testament as they worked closely together (Acts 18:5; 19:22), coauthored books of the Bible (2 Cor. 1:1; Phil. 1:1; Col. 1:1; 1 Thess. 1:1; 2 Thess. 1:1), and served God side by side (1 Cor. 4:17; 16:10; Rom. 16:21). Occasionally, however, they were separated because Paul would send Timothy on important missions to straighten out problems that arose in various local churches (e.g., 1 Thess. 3:1–6).

Paul and Timothy gave their lives to serving Jesus Christ by serving his bride, the church. They were acutely aware of the various problems in local churches, but rather than standing at a distance to criticize the church, they threw themselves into the needs of churches and served tirelessly. These men loved the church so dearly because they were following the example of Jesus. Jesus died for the sins of his church (Eph. 5:25); he is the Apostle who plants churches (Heb. 3:1); he is head over the church (Eph. 5:23); he is senior pastor in the church (1 Peter 5:4), and he is the builder of the church (Matt. 16:18). Jesus simply loves the church, and because Paul and Timothy loved Jesus, they, too, loved the church.

On one of his missionary journeys, Paul planted the first church in Ephesus (Acts 19). Before finally leaving Ephesus for the last time, Paul gave a stern warning to the elders/pastors of the Ephesian church that false teachers would rise up from within the church and try to destroy it after he departed (Acts 20). After warning the leaders of the tough job that lay ahead of them, Paul prayed for the Ephesian elders as they shed many tears over his departure, knowing they would not see him again until they met one day in heaven.

After Paul's departure, the troubles and troublemakers that Paul prophesied would come to Ephesus began to emerge. Young Timothy, laboring in Ephesus to sort out a litany of church problems, was apparently in a bit over his head. Subsequently, Paul wrote Timothy two letters—1 and 2 Timothy—in an effort to encourage and direct his friend. Unlike the other New Testament letters, which are written to churches, these letters and a similar letter to Titus are very personal correspondences from an older pastor to individual young leaders whom he was mentoring.

Though the letters of 1–2 Timothy are quite similar in many respects, they do have some important differences. For example, in both letters Paul is gravely concerned about the condition of the church and Timothy. In 1 Timothy, Paul is concerned *primar-*

ily with the well-being of the church and *secondarily* with the well-being of his friend Timothy. In 2 Timothy, though, the tone and content of the letter reveal that Paul's concerns have flipped, as he is primarily concerned with Timothy's welfare. Though still obviously pained by the heretics and the effects of their demonic doctrines in the church, they are treated as a secondary matter. This is why 2 Timothy is one of the most personal, intimate, reflective, emotional, and pastoral sections of the entire Bible. Every pastor needs a pastor, and the young pastor Timothy had Paul.

Second Timothy is likely the last letter that Paul penned. It may have been written only days before he was murdered by beheading at the hands of the godless megalomaniac emperor Nero (4:6–7). Paul didn't go out with his head down and voice trembling, though. Second Timothy is a courageous, triumphant final shout from Paul about his coming entrance into God's kingdom (4:18), where he would receive his final reward for being a faithful minister of the gospel. He didn't flinch, even in the face of death (4:7–8). To enter into the passion and beauty of Paul's final letter, it will be helpful for you to see Paul sitting alone in a dark, dank cell, rubbing the aching joints on his body scarred by frequent beatings, not whining about his lot or cursing God for his demise, but rather maintaining his steely-eyed gaze, determined to leave this world with his boots on, head high, and mouth singing the praises of his Lord, Jesus. History records they chopped off his head because it was the only way to silence him.

Before dying, Paul wrote 2 Timothy to express his deep affection for his faithful friend and co-laborer of fifteen years. He also wanted to ensure that his ministry would continue after his death, by younger Christians taking the baton from his hand and running for Christ with reckless abandon, pulling people in their wake as he had. Therefore, to benefit from 2 Timothy we must be set aflame by the same Holy Spirit who lived in Paul and burn brightly for Jesus as he did.

Only then can we heed his commands not to be timid or ashamed of Jesus, but rather fight like a soldier, compete like an athlete, and work like a farmer. Only then can we lovingly encourage faithful people like Onesiphorus, Priscilla, Aquila, Erastus, Trophimus, Eubulus, Pudens, Linus, and Claudia as he did. Only then can we courageously oppose heretics and servants of Satan such as Hymenaeus, Philetus, and Demas as he did. Only then can we train and empower faithful leaders of God's church and faithful teachers of God's Word as he commanded.

Our hope in studying 2 Timothy is that we would stand alongside Timothy as part of Paul's legacy of faithful servants of Jesus Christ, who have been the beneficiaries of his mentorship. To do so we must avoid wasting time on stupid arguments with spiritually diseased fools (2:14–16), not join sinners in their rebellion (3:1–9), accept hardship as part of faithful Christian life (3:10–15), hold our Bibles high while humbly standing under them (3:16–17), and be inspired and rebuked by the preaching of God's Word (4:1–4) so that lost people around us will be saved by God as he works through us (4:5). And indeed we shall, because Jesus goes with us and brings his grace (4:22).

NEUTRALS, NEGATIVES, AND POSITIVES

Like every ministry leader invariably experiences, Timothy found himself in a battle. Those who I like to call "negatives" had infiltrated the church. Paul goes so far as to call out the chief negatives by name, Hymenaeus and Philetus, who were the leaders of painful strife and division in the church. And like every ministry leader painfully knows, such negatives are never alone but rather become the lightning rod for every disgruntled, disillusioned, and dangerous person in the church.

Worse still, like a cancer rapidly spreading throughout the church body, the "neutrals" were being drawn into the conflict, which is what Paul means when he says in 2 Timothy 2:18, "They are upsetting the faith of some." These kinds of situations are nothing short of exhausting. Timothy would have been undoubtedly overwhelmed with a range of emotions from despair to concern and even righteous anger. The number of people asking to meet with him would have filled his calendar, distracting him from time for study, prayer, preaching, Sabbath, evangelism, and the like. Subsequently, Paul's loving letter came at an opportune time. Paul was seasoned in remaining positive and leading neutrals in the face of opposition from negatives, and he instructs Timothy how to stay positive as well.

Because Paul's words are divinely inspired, they are timeless, which makes them ever timely. Ministry leaders need to be "positive." They also need to know who the positives, negatives, and neutrals are (both in official leadership and unofficial leadership) in their ministries.

Positives

Positives are people who do gospel-things in gospel-ways for gospel-reasons. They are trusting, supportive, and encouraging. They build bridges and mediate conflict. Positives bring organizational health, work for the good of the gospel over any single issue or cause, and are a blessing because they humbly want the gospel to win. Positives are prone to turn neutrals into positives, while they also work to neutralize negatives. In the Bible, positives are often referred to as shepherds.

Negatives

Negatives are people who do ungospel-things in ungospel-ways for ungospel-reasons. They are distrusting, unsupportive, discouraging, and contentious. They burn bridges, are wounded by bitterness from past hurts, and are often the source of criticism and conflict. Negatives bring organizational sickness, division, and trouble because they are more interested in proudly winning their cause than in the triumph of the gospel and the good of the whole church. Negatives tend to draw other negatives toward themselves as factions; they also prey on neutrals in order to increase their own power and control. In the Bible, negatives are often referred to as wolves.

There are about as many kinds of negatives as there are types of sins. Some notable negatives include these:

1. Success-jealousy negatives snipe and criticize because they covet your ministry, covet your success, and/or covet God's grace in your life.
2. False-witness negatives spread lies or "half-truths" about others.
3. Misinformed negatives criticize, complain, whine, or perhaps just become passive out of ignorance or susceptibility to wrong information.
4. Personal-dislike negatives equate distaste for the pastor's tone, style, personality type, sense of humor, and so forth, with appraisal of his character or ministry qualification.
5. Take-up-offense-for-another-person negatives are always willing to make someone else a martyr or relay anonymous grapevine chatter on behalf of someone who allegedly can't or won't speak for themselves.
6. Missiological negatives are Christians who either on the right, rather like fundamentalists, disengage from culture and practice ecclesiological isolationism, or on the left, like liberals, shave off fidelity to the gospel and to the authority of Scripture in their efforts to be more culturally acceptable.
7. Single-issue-voter negatives view the gospel as Jesus *plus something else,* typically something political or cultural like voting Republican or Democrat, homeschooling, or saving the planet

ecologically, but sometimes their issues are more theological like KJV-onlyism or the regulative principle.

8. Little-world negatives do not feel any sense of urgency for hurting and lost neighbors but are distrustful of anything or anyone outside of their proverbial church community, theological faction, denominational affiliation, favorite publishing house offering, political party, or other idol that has obscured their view of God's kingdom.

9. Chain-of-command negatives want more than anything to be at the top. And if they can't be at the top, they want access to the top. They don't obey the chain of command of church leadership, but presume and press, appointing themselves the person at whom the buck stops and demanding to be heard whenever they deem their opinion important.

10. Tradition negatives are anti-change.

11. Unforgiving negatives are mired in bitterness and keep retrieving the same old rocks they have thrown repeatedly, just so they can throw them again.

12. Plank-speck negatives like to preach repentance without actually practicing it, while conveniently overlooking their own sin as they judge others.

13. Diotrephes-negatives are like their forefather in 3 John who apparently employed a two-pronged affront consisting of slandering the character of ministry leaders and seeking to keep neutrals away from the positives. They want to be known; they want to be listed on the literature; they want to be honored; they want to be publicly thanked. They don't want Jesus to be first because they want to be first.

14. Distrust negatives are cynical, suspicious, hard for a leader to win their trust, and even harder for a leader to keep their trust.

15. Control negatives prefer to wield power rather than influence by working through church politics, stall tactics, and other passive-aggressive ways to lead without being a leader.

16. Critic negatives are the hall monitors of church life. They love to nitpick and dig up dirt, no matter how minuscule, and are good at keeping a record of wrongs.

17. Warrior negatives have zeal that usually knows no bounds and are always looking for the next hill to die on.

18. One-handed negatives put everything either in the open hand of flexibility (liberals) or closed hand of inflexibility (fundamentalists). Lacking discernment to know what goes in the open and

closed hands, they are constantly half-right and half-wrong, which makes them always a problem.

19. Gossip negatives are always talking *about* others but never talking *to* them, often outlandishly doing this in the name of prayer.

20. Theological negatives are the heretics, apostates, and other various theological wing nuts who have an appetite for error.

This is just a sampling of the negatives challenging positive ministry and threatening the security of the neutrals in a church. There are more than are listed, even combinations of the individual negatives above, that make pastoral ministry the dangerous frontlines of the church's work in advancing the kingdom of God. I offer them as some examples of the pain of pastoral work. Tragically, too many criticisms of the church and books written about the church come from those who are not covered in the blood and mud of the spiritual warfare that rages in a local church, and as such are prone to idealism instead of realism, employing bumper sticker slogans for complex sin problems.

As a young pastor likely under the age of forty (1 Tim. 4:12; 2 Tim. 2:22), Timothy would have been literally fighting for the life of the gospel and the church entrusted to his leadership, because Hymenaeus and Philetus could have pulled all of the various negatives in the church at Ephesus into one deadly faction. Without Paul present to help, Timothy was overwhelmed, exhausted, frustrated, agitated, and likely tempted to react in a sinful way rather than respond in a sanctified way. To make matters worse, Timothy was prone to ongoing illness and possibly intestinal problems caused, at least in part, by the stress of his ministry (1 Tim. 5:23). He needed Paul to help him stay positive for the sake of the neutrals who were hanging in the balance and capable of becoming positives or negatives.

Neutrals

Neutrals are Christians at varying stages of their sanctification who are not leaders but rather easily influenced followers. These impressionable people are prone to being unsure, confused, and fearful, depending upon what information they are given and who they are in relationship with. Neutrals are often caught in the middle when there is conflict between positives and negatives. A neutral becomes a positive or negative depending upon who their friends are, who they listen to, what information they have access to, what books they read, and which teachers they trust.

Change is controversial. It requires someone who is a strong positive to build consensus for change, and who is also able to neutralize the negatives rather than being influenced by them. Paul is both warning the neutrals not to give into the negatives, and supporting Timothy's leadership by writing 1–2 Timothy, knowing that his words, carrying apostolic authority, would be read to the church. In this example we learn that when a church has become altogether toxic, the outside counsel of a godly and wise pastor is incredibly helpful. Cancerous members of the church body are to be carefully cut out with such surgical skill that will prevent their disease from spreading until it kills the church body, and also keep their removal from causing a hemorrhage, thereby also killing the church body.

PAUL'S CHARGING OF TIMOTHY

Paul isn't just encouraging Timothy or even instructing him. In his letters, with apostolic authority and the transmission of God's perfect life-giving Word, he is imparting grace to the embattled young pastor. The whole of Paul's work serves as a positive charge to Timothy. Paul positively instructs Timothy, saying in 2 Timothy 2:14–26:

Remind them of these things, and charge them before God not to quarrel about words, which does no good, but only ruins the hearers. Do your best to present yourself to God as one approved, a worker who has no need to be ashamed, rightly handling the word of truth. But avoid irreverent babble, for it will lead people into more and more ungodliness, and their talk will spread like gangrene. Among them are Hymenaeus and Philetus, who have swerved from the truth, saying that the resurrection has already happened. They are upsetting the faith of some. But God's firm foundation stands, bearing this seal: "The Lord knows those who are his," and, "Let everyone who names the name of the Lord depart from iniquity."

Now in a great house there are not only vessels of gold and silver but also of wood and clay, some for honorable use, some for dishonorable. Therefore, if anyone cleanses himself from what is dishonorable, he will be a vessel for honorable use, set apart as holy, useful to the master of the house, ready for every good work.

So flee youthful passions and pursue righteousness, faith, love, and peace, along with those who call on the Lord from a pure heart. Have nothing to do with foolish, ignorant controversies; you know that they breed quarrels. And the Lord's servant must not be quarrelsome but kind to everyone, able to teach, patiently enduring evil, correcting his opponents with gentleness. God may perhaps grant them repentance leading to a knowledge of the truth, and they may come to their senses and escape from the snare of the devil, after being captured by him to do his will.

There are a few negatives mentioned in this passage and some implied.

Sadly, in most ministries, the negatives are the most vocal, most exhausting, and most distracting. They are also the least likely to contribute to the growth and health of the church. Though they are few, they are often loud and difficult, spreading like gangrene through the church body (2 Tim. 2:17). Practically, this means that even a few negatives working together can become quite problematic. The Bible reveals that negatives often pair up like two barrels on a gun, as was the case with Jannes

and Jambres opposing Moses, Sanballat and Tobiah opposing Nehemiah, Hymenaeus and Alexander opposing Paul, and
Hymenaeus and Philetus opposing Timothy.

For a ministry to remain positive, three things need to occur.
First, the senior leader and the other official and unofficial leaders who wield the most influence must be positives. Furthermore,
they must be continually exhorted to remain positives. This
means that even when they deal with negative things, they do so
in a positive way for the glory of God and the good of his people.
This is what Paul is exhorting Timothy to learn amidst his fiery
trial in 2 Timothy 2:14–26.

Second, the negatives must not be allowed into leadership. If they are in leadership, official or unofficial, they must
be rebuked. Too often negatives are tolerated for too long;
the longer their sin is tolerated, the more toxic the ministry-
culture becomes. Therefore, unrepentant negatives need to be
brought through formal church discipline after their negativ-
ity has been documented and addressed; this process may end
with their removal from the ministry, if necessary. Ministry
leaders are often reticent to deal so forthrightly with negatives; however, the longer they are tolerated, the more neutrals
they infect with their "gangrene" (2 Tim. 2:17). Paul models
for Timothy and all ministry leaders how to deal with unholy,
unofficial leaders by naming and rebuking them, speaking of
"Hymenaeus and Philetus, who have swerved from the truth"
(2 Tim. 2:17–18).

Third, the neutrals need to be lovingly and patiently informed
that they are neutrals and that they need to take responsibility
not to give in to negatives. Additionally, neutrals cannot be
allowed into ministry leadership because they are prone to be
influenced rather than be influencers. Sadly, neutrals are often

nominated for and voted in to ministry leadership because they tend to be nice and likeable people, since they are amiable and easily influenced. The problem is that they are prone to work toward consensus rather than lead and are therefore not helpful for moving a ministry forward into innovation and growth.

What Paul says to Timothy in 2 Timothy 2:14–26 creates a theological rationale (honorable, dishonorable) and a gracious tone (gentle, kind) for the necessary work of shooting the wolves that threaten the sheep.

But we don't have to go between the lines to read how to do this. Paul is quite clear.

MARKS OF POSITIVE MINISTRY

For as many negatives as there are, the blessings of positives are even greater. The kingdom will be advanced because Jesus will build his church. For the sake of the neutrals (and for the sake of the repentance of negatives), the Scriptures equip us with more than enough ministry positives.

What does it take to pastor positively? Paul specifies twenty markers in 2 Timothy 2:14–26, from which we can see the shape of positive leadership.

1. Positively emphasize what you are for, not what you're against.

Second Timothy 2:14 begins, "Remind them of these things." What things? All that has come before in the text. Following the trajectory of Paul's exhortation to Timothy throughout the entire letter, we see that 14–26 is the practical conclusion of the doxological confession coming before it, culminating in the gospel-suffering that immediately precedes the passage at hand. Paul writes this in 2:10–13:

Therefore I endure everything for the sake of the elect, that they also may obtain the salvation that is in Christ Jesus with eternal glory. The saying is trustworthy, for:

> *If we have died with him, we will also live with him;*
> *if we endure, we will also reign with him;*
> *if we deny him, he also will deny us;*
> *if we are faithless, he remains faithful—*

for he cannot deny himself.

This is what we must tenaciously bring to the minds of our church communities. God's covenantal faithfulness is the *a priori* of the Christian life, the "thesis statement" from which we may convincingly argue against gossip, silly talk, lies, heresies, and the like.

There are two important foundations in verses 10–13 for the general admonition toward positive ministry in verses 14–26. The first is that if we have died with Christ, we ought to live with him (v. 11), which means our community life, our speech, our interactions and relationships, and our attraction to spiritual things ought to reflect the life Christ gives, not the death that separation from him reflects. If the shape of our community conversation is divisiveness and departure from the faith, we have not truly died with Christ. The second foundation is the general initiative of the gospel. If we are centered on the good news, we would not as a result be "bad news-ing" each other.

Our fundamentalist forebears are guilty on this point, and their children would be well served to repent of the sins of their spiritual fathers. They began with a good focus on the fundamentals of sound doctrine and then expanded their focus to so much more and inadvertently began to give up ground. By emphasizing all sorts of open hand, second-tier issues like alcohol, movies and television and music, political advancement, and the like, they failed to hold the gospel of Jesus Christ as their greatest treasure and source of their comfort, hope, and identity. In a word, they failed to fix their eyes solely on Jesus and got distracted. They fell into the trap of word-quarrels and ignorant controversies, and we have been cleaning up their (our!) mess ever since. This is what happens when you identify yourself more by what you're against than what you're for.

Quarrels over words (v. 14), mishandling the Scriptures (v. 15), irreverent babble and ungodliness (v. 16), heresy (vv. 17–18), sin (v. 19), and ignorant controversies (v. 23) all result when the gospel has not set the tone of conversation. The tongues of negatives can be a hellish fire,[1] spreading like a wild blaze until we can orient neutrals around the gospel. As Luther writes, "Most necessary it is therefore, that we should know this article well, teach it unto others, and beat it into their heads continually."[2] Faithfully preaching the "first importance" of the gospel (1 Cor. 15:3) is the first step in preparing neutrals for positive transformation.

2. Positively use your God-given authority.

"Charge them before God," Paul continues in verse 14. This is the godly counterclaim against those who are susceptible to warring about minutiae. To guard them from their own penchant for rhetorical infighting, positive leaders must fight for gospel-centrality and doctrinal soundness. "Warn them," the NIV says. Gently throw your pastoral weight around; use your bully pulpit. Remind them and *charge* them before the almighty God to honor him and his work with their mouths. While soft words produce hard people, hard words produce soft people. Truly loving ministry leaders will not just give their people soft words while

---

[1] James 3:6.
[2] Martin Luther, *A Commentary on Saint Paul's Epistle to the Galatians* (Cambridge, MA: Harvard, 1844), 103.

reserving their hard words for the sins of other people outside the church. No, in love they will also use hard words to call their people to repent of their own spiritual pride, sin, and selfishness so that they may be soft toward God and others.

Control-negatives and tradition-negatives in particular can benefit from a firm reminder of pastoral authority. If not an arrogant pulling of rank, a gentle reminder from a place of humble authority can actually jostle people away from their presumption or power trip. Sometimes all disorder needs is a loud call to order.

3. Positively invest your words.

What do we charge them to do? We charge them before God, verse 14 reads, "not to quarrel about words, which does no good, but only ruins the hearers." Because Paul qualifies the word-quarrels here as something that ruins hearers and because Paul has been willing over and over to contend for the faith, he is not suggesting that debate and vigorous dialogue are off-limits when the claims of the Christian faith are at stake. If he meant that, he would not have kicked Hymenaeus and Alexander out of the church, but would have just rolled over and considered the unchallenged spread of their destruction better than "quarreling" with them. But that's not what he means.

No, positively contending for the faith builds up the hearers. It is good for the bedrock of Christian belief. What Paul aims at here is perhaps endless disputes over second- and third-tier issues. We have heard the urban legends of modern churches that split over what color carpet should be installed in the fellowship hall. Churches have actually split over music styles and Bible translation choices. Picture a new Christian or curious non-Christian in the middle of such division. What would an inability to reconcile over such comparatively minute matters communicate to neutrals about (a) what is of first importance and (b) what Christian community is for? How many hearers have ever been ruined by such quarrels in your own ministry? What quarrelers believe is at stake is their own reputation and their own selfish victories. Meanwhile we compromise what really matters.

The word for "ruins" in verse 14 is *katastrophé*, which as its appearance indicates, is "the opposite of edification."[3] One of the marks of positive leadership is that it invests its words well, seeking the building up of the church body and the transmission of the hope of the gospel, and if damage must be done, such effort should be exerted toward powers and personalities who are set against the advancement of the kingdom and the worship of the King.

4. Positively do your best.

"Do your best to present yourself to God as one approved," Paul continues in verse 15. This does not refer to the so-called "excellence" that has become an idol in many churches. It does not mean that we only do positive things in positive ways while wearing a positively dazzling smile so that our words bear little resemblance to the double-edged sword that is God's Word. Rather, Paul is encouraging Timothy to get his hands dirty doing the hard work of pastoral ministry.

Paul is no demanding perfectionist, but he is exhorting Timothy to "do his best." The emphasis is on diligence, with the intended aim of not needing to be ashamed; the intention is not directly on results. In Paul's spiritual economy, we give the sweat, and God gives the results.

With that in mind, with the measurement being done before God, doing one's best does not mean working for the approval

---

[3]Thomas D. Lea and Hayne P. Griffin Jr., *1, 2 Timothy, Titus*, The New American Commentary (Nashville: Broadman, 1992), 214.

or applause of men. One of the worst things a pastor can do is become a people-pleaser. It is dangerously easy to drift into this, and it doesn't always happen for sinful reasons. When a pastor plays to a faction in his church because they are big givers or carry the influence of their position in life or in the history of the church, he is becoming a spiritual prostitute. But when he plays to a faction or a person out of just not wanting to hurt their feelings, his intentions are admirable. They're just not necessarily pastoral. A positive will do his best for God, seeking God's approval and alignment with God's will, and then let the cards fall where they may with the people.

5. Positively work hard.

Unashamed workmanship is a cohort of standing approved before God. Paul urges Timothy in verse 15 to become "a worker who has no need to be ashamed." This is the behavioral antidote to shameful quarrels and divisiveness—working hard in the blessing of a pure conscience. "The best medicine against the disease of 'disputes about words' is Timothy's good conduct itself."[4]

The word "worker" is repeatedly employed elsewhere in reference to an agricultural worker, which is not only a great reflection of the pastoral work of leaders but to what is involved in a pastoral work ethic that one need not be ashamed of—weed-pulling, diligence, patience, longsuffering, expectation, prayer, gentleness. While the negatives may work hard at disturbing the peace, positives must work hard to preserve and restore it. Positives cannot afford to be caught slacking off; we must stand guard over our ministries with vigilance, like Nehemiah's workers with a sword in one hand to defend the work and a trowel in another to do the work (Neh. 4:17b).

---

[4]M. Dibelius and H. Conzelmann, *The Pastoral Epistles* (Philadelphia: Fortress, 1972), 111.

6. Positively study harder.

Part and parcel of doing one's best and working hard is "rightly handling the word of truth" (v. 15). This study in fact is the primary way positives demonstrate doing their best and working their hardest. This passage shortly precedes Paul's reminder, "All Scripture is breathed out by God and profitable for teaching, for reproof, for correction, and for training in righteousness, that the man of God may be competent, equipped for every good work" (2 Tim. 3:16–17).

The word translated "rightly handling" in verse 15 is "a metaphor that literally means 'to cut straight,'"[5] bringing to mind a physical cutting (though whether of wood or stone or fabric we can only guess). It is an apt metaphor for the pastor seeking to cultivate a Word-shaped community, for whom and in which "cutting" in matters of life and doctrine is vitally important. At the risk of dulling this sharp metaphor, perhaps we may also say that a pastor who is rightly handling the Word of truth always shoots straight. He does not waffle on biblical truth but is passionate and honest about it. You always know where he stands, which is to say, on "the word of truth." Such a positive, proactive stance is a hearty antidote to vain disputations, gossip, and outright heresy, because while the neutrals may be at risk from the negatives, echoing the Serpentine "Did God really say . . . ?" (Gen. 3:1, NIV), they have the assurance that their pastor will always be a serious student and truth-teller.

In addition, studying harder because of the challenges of negatives is a great cause of refinement in the doctrinal integrity of a community. The negatives can become an ironic blessing as they push positives to know the Word of God better. It is because of negatives that the church eventually developed the

---

[5]Gordon D. Fee, *1 and 2 Timothy, Titus*, New International Biblical Commentary (San Francisco: Harper & Row, 1984), 205.

positives of solid theology, the classic creeds, and stronger, healthier churches.[6]

7. Positively avoid getting drawn into endless arguments.

Second Timothy 2:16–17 says, "But avoid irreverent babble, for it will lead people into more and more ungodliness, and their talk will spread like gangrene." The word in verse 17 translated "gangrene" is "a disease involving severe inflammation, which if left unchecked can become a destructive ulcerous condition."[7] Besides "gangrene," the lexicographers list "cancer" as another possible translation.

The word "spread" is an idiom meaning "to have pasture."[8] The thrust is still that of the spreading decay of flesh from rot or infection, both in the meaning of this idiom and in the contextual connection Paul makes to gangrene (or cancer), but pastors should not short shrift the "have pasture" literalism. Leaders set the tone for the personality of their communities; they lead the setting up of conditions that either foster health or disease. Whatever conditions we cultivate in our sheep pens will create a healthy or an unhealthy flock. This means we shepherds must diligently monitor and direct whatever "has pasture" in our pastures.

And that means not being drawn into ridiculous arguments, gossipy babble, and assorted other vain disputations, but instead setting the conversational tone by instigating positive speech and initiating gospel-driven proclamation in word and deed (e.g., preaching the core truths of sin and grace and further enacting the gospel truth by repenting, forgiving, and counseling others toward like-minded reconciliation). Take the initiative in babble-

---

[6]This is related to the "honorable/dishonorable" discussion below.
[7]BAGD, 186.
[8]Lea and Griffin, *1, 2 Timothy, Titus*, 216.

avoidance by creating a community-wide conversation that honors God, draws in neutrals, and repels negatives. Positively declaring both the sovereignty of God and the invitation to sinners to repent and believe the gospel, for instance, can do a world of good in shutting up militant Calvinists and ignorant Arminians. Calvin's call to be proactive is wise:

> Since the disease is so destructive we must treat it early on and not wait until it has established a hold, for then it will be too late to counter it. The terrible extinction of the Gospel among the Roman Catholics came about because, through the ignorance and the sloth of the pastors, corruptions prevailed unchecked for a long time and gradually destroyed the purity of doctrine.[9]

8. Positively warn the sheep of the wolves.

Who are the wolves? In verses 17–18, Paul names names: "Among them are Hymenaeus and Philetus, who have swerved from the truth, saying that the resurrection has already happened. They are upsetting the faith of some."

Back in the prequel to the present epistle, Paul deals with Hymenaeus and a buddy who's with him named Alexander (1 Tim. 1:18–20). Hymenaeus had infiltrated the church, bringing with him false doctrine. Paul writes in 1 Timothy 1:20 that he has handed them "over to Satan that they may learn not to blaspheme." Paul is confident that Hymenaeus is not teachable. He's not flexible; he's not submissive. Consequently, he's ruining people's faith. Hymenaeus represents a disease, a cancer in the church that just continues to spread. And like a gangrenous limb, he must be amputated from the body.

Occasionally, positive leaders must remove people from the church. In my ministry, we've done that on a few occasions

---

[9]John Calvin, *1 and 2 Timothy and Titus,* Crossway Classic Commentaries, ed. J. I. Packer and Alister McGrath (Wheaton, IL: Crossway, 1998), 139.

with people who are not teachable, who want to be teachers but are very pushy, and who instigate godless chatter. They are Diotrephes-negatives or chain-of-command negatives. And their teaching spreads like gangrene. Other people end up getting sick. And more painful and deadly than removing them is not removing them.

In 2 Timothy, Hymenaeus is still a problem, but does he even attend that church? No. Didn't Paul excommunicate him? Yes. So why wasn't Hymenaeus neutralized? Kelly writes, "We cannot assume that the Apostle's ban was instantaneously effective in silencing a heretic, and indeed the fact that Hymenaeus could apparently ignore it illustrates the difficult situation in the Ephesian church."[10] We can imagine Hymenaeus opening his home and inviting church members over to hear his case against Paul and Timothy, shedding tears, and pleading for their support, perhaps even while family lamented the pain they suffered because of their removal from the church as an attempt to abuse Christian compassion for demonic deception.

This is why protecting the neutrals is so important—because negatives don't play fairly or nicely. Yes, Paul kicked Hymenaeus out of the church, but he is still a problem in the church. This is what false teachers do. They leverage any lingering, remaining relationships, trying to convert people to their belief structure as an entry point back into the body. That's how Satan works. That's how he worked with Judas. He was thinking, "If I can get one guy on the team, I can try and take down the whole team."

A key area of discernment for positives is being very, very careful with whom you lead as friends. This rarely has anything to do with friends who are not believers. Non-Christians, quite frankly, are hardly ever the problem. Paul warns in Acts 20:30

---

[10]J. N. D. Kelly, *A Commentary on the Pastoral Epistles* (Grand Rapids: Baker, 1981), 184.

that men will arise from your own number and distort the truth and lead many astray. The most dangerous threats to your church are already inside your church or just outside its doors on the way in.

One characteristic of neutrals is that they are, well, *neutral*. They have no opinion about the carriers of heterodox doctrine preying on their minds. Picture a new Christian, for instance, unwise in the ways of theology. He or she may see a purveyor of prosperity and bankrupt spirituality on television or have one of their ilk recommended by a less discerning Christian friend. He or she doesn't have the framework to determine whether these characters are worth listening to. Before you know it, this new Christian has been taken captive by a winsome personality, a dynamic speaking style, or an overly cheerful message. By contrast, a positive who is warning against such things can come across angry, judgmental, and grumpy—like a negative! So it is important to warn the sheep about the wolves regularly, to prepare them to know the wolves are out there, and to equip them to identify them.

Be specific. Just as Paul names names here, don't be afraid to, in the appropriate settings, name the heresies, name the quarrels, name the temptations, and perhaps even name the parties involved. If that seems uncomfortable to you, imagine how uncomfortable it will be to find out that neutrals have been led away from the faith or into spiritual despair because of your passivity and failure to warn them.

9. Positively rejoice that God rules the church.

Second Timothy 2:19 begins, "But God's firm foundation stands, bearing this seal: 'The Lord knows those who are his.'"

The encouragement here is twofold. First, we are assured

of God's faithfulness, of the comfort of his loving sovereignty. Christ will build his church. You will fail to be positive often. But the building of the kingdom does not rise or fall on you. The "but" implies that even if we fail to live up to the previous positive markers as perfectly as possible, we can in no way hinder God's will. We cannot thwart him, neither intentionally or inadvertently. His foundation, which is strong, will stand.

The second encouragement is the assurance of foreknowledge and election. And this encouragement is itself twofold. It tells us that we are owned by God; it is a good gospel-word of assurance to positives whose positivity isn't foolproof. And it is an assurance that no one can snatch God's elect out of his hand. He will have them. The "inscription" referred to is the "secret" seal of salvation, securing the eternal destiny of those whom God foreknows.[11] So even as we contend for the faith, we do not contend as if the results hinge on us, but as though the results hinge on God despite his using of us to proclaim his truth and righteousness in Christ.

10. Positively practice repentance before preaching it.

Second Timothy 2:19 continues, "Let everyone who names the name of the Lord depart from iniquity." Positives set the example. Double honor (1 Tim. 5:17) calls for double responsibility, does it not? You cannot call others to gospel-brokenness if you do not regularly practice it yourself. The Bible calls that hypocrisy. Your sin will find you out, and leaders do not get a free pass on the daily work of taking up their cross.

This is of critical importance. God's Word will not return void (Isa. 55:11), and Paul affirms that the gospel preached even

---

[11]Calvin, *1 and 2 Timothy*, 140.

from impure motives will bring God glory (Phil. 1:18). But you will herald the gospel most effectively when you stand in awe and thankful need of it yourself. The preaching of repentance by one who still clings to his sin is like the alcoholic preaching against porn addiction. It is the classic game, plank-speck religion. If you're going to preach the cross, make sure its beams are not stuck in your eye.

Preach repentance positively by practicing it regularly. The reality is that if you do not find ways to develop humility within yourself, God will find more ways to do it by allowing you to enjoy humiliation, which is always the alternate plan for the proud.

11. Positively use your passion to be a better servant.

In 2 Timothy 2:20–21, Paul launches into an extended metaphor with multiple implications. His illustration begins this way:

> *Now in a great house there are not only vessels of gold and silver but also of wood and clay, some for honorable use, some for dishonorable. Therefore, if anyone cleanses himself from what is dishonorable, he will be a vessel for honorable use, set apart as holy, useful to the master of the house, ready for every good work.*

In the sterling dichotomous tradition of sheep and goats, wheat and chaff, and even Paul's own "not all who are descended from Israel belong to Israel" (Rom. 9:6), he develops an excursus on vessels for honorable and dishonorable use. Guthrie writes:

> The illustration in vv. 20–21 continues the building metaphor in v. 19. But Paul now concentrates on the utensils used in a great house. The various materials out of which they are made stand for different purposes, some noble, others ignoble. The application here is some-what confused, for wooden vessels are as necessary

as golden and in fact are more frequently used. But Paul thinks of Christian workers as precious in God's sight. Yet what does Paul mean by cleansing from ignoble use? Perhaps the best explanation is that Paul is still thinking of Hymenaeus and Philetus (cf. 1 Cor. 5:7 for a parallel use of the verb meaning "to purge or cleanse").[12]

Paul's illustrative dichotomy in just a few choice words establishes the "need" for the dual presence of honorable vessels and dishonorable vessels. Some translations may interpret "dishonorable" or "ignoble" more in terms of "ordinary," but the sense here is not, for instance, of bowls that are for impressing company and bowls used every day when it's just family, but rather bowls that are for eating food out of and bowls that are for sitting on . . . sort of. "More likely garbage or excrement is in view."[13]

At my house I have a barbecue grill upon which the great man-trinity of fire, meat, and sauce gather in joyous unison. Also at my house, I have a toilet. Next to the toilet I have a plunger and a brush. The brush is a lot like the barbecue brush outside by my grill, and if turned upside down the plunger holds roughly the same amount of liquid as my barbecue sauce bowl. The brush for the toilet bowl has a long handle and so does my barbecue brush. Theoretically, you could use the toilet brush and plunger to marinate a rack of ribs, but you wouldn't want to. You probably see where I'm going with this.

These parallels are actually in view in the text. There are brushes for marinating meat and for cleaning toilets. There are bowls that hold barbecue sauce and plungers that could be used to do the same. Of course, it would be unwise to not notice and abide by this distinction in function.

---

[12]Donald Guthrie, "2 Timothy," in *New Bible Commentary, 21st Century Edition*, 4th ed. (Downers Grove, IL: InterVarsity, 1994), 1307–8.
[13]Fee, *1 and 2 Timothy, Titus*, 211.

But that doesn't mean I don't need the toilet brush and the plunger. You need both. That's what Paul is saying. Heretics in the church are like toilet brushes and plungers. In the church, just like in the toilet, some things collect that would be better to pass. There are certain doctrines, attitudes, and laissez-faire sorts of apathetic theologies floating around. People don't read their Bibles, so they don't grow. They're indifferent, and all of a sudden a little bit of funk starts to settle in. It gets a little stinky in the church. When you get such buildup, you suddenly need a brush and a plunger. And God says, "I'll send you some. Hymenaeus and Philetus, plunger and brush. Here they come."

This sounds silly, but the connection is important. Why would God let them in the church? The answer is to serve in the church's cleansing. This is an echo of the positive work of hard study resulting from the challenge of vain disputations and heresies. Persistent dirt challenges you to get better at cleaning. When you are attacked by a heretic, you read your Bible like never before. When the heretic is not there, you may be tempted to be lazy with the Scriptures and apathetic about doctrine. You may be lazy and indifferent with lots of stinky buildup, and then all of a sudden the heretic comes in and starts causing a fuss.

Throughout the history of the church, God has taken stinky churches and stinky Christians and brought heretics to them. He doesn't make people be heretics, but he'll direct them to those places where they're most needed. They will insinuate themselves into the church. A church led by positives, for the sake of the neutrals, will respond by cleansing itself and flushing these negatives out. This process is, believe it or not, healthy for the church. Or at the very least, it makes a church healthier.

12. Positively grow up quickly.

"So flee youthful passions," Paul instructs Timothy in verse 22. The Bible basically says nothing positive about young men except that they're strong. But so are terrorists.

The problem with vain disputations and quasi-heresies and quarrels over words is that they are tempting bait for young men. Nobody loves arguing over open-hand theological issues like young men. There is something about the intellectual and emotional dawn of masculine maturation that instinctively draws young guys to stupid arguments. And many times the issues and topics are good things—things we should have opinions on or enjoy discussing. But young men are like Bambi on the frozen pond—all awkward limbs and little coordination.

Young leaders, you must be very, very careful. You must actively seek out the deeper maturity of doctrinal soundness in peace and gentility. Seek mentors in older believers as Timothy did with Paul, rather than with fellow young men.

Some seem to think that Paul is challenging Timothy's timidity. That may be so, but it is not timidity that Paul is warning his protégé away from here but "passions." Timothy has all the zeal of youth, and Paul wants to make sure he channels it honorably, that he does not follow his impulses into unholiness.

This is not about looking down on youthfulness (as Paul instructs Timothy not to let anyone do in 1 Tim. 4:12). It is about seeing your own youthfulness realistically and then proactively seeking the maturity and wisdom of the Scriptures, traditions, and Christian leaders who have gone before you. It is about not being subject to your attitudes and impulses but actively creating conditions that will help you subject your attitudes and impulses to the Spirit. If you are young, who do you submit to? Who corrects you? Who are you accountable to?

13. Positively seek righteousness, faith, love,
and peace with urgency.

Paul continues his exhortation to "flee youthful passions"
in verse 22 with the further command to "pursue righteousness, faith, love, and peace, along with those who call on the
Lord from a pure heart." This is a positive pursuit of positive
spirituality. The indication here is that these traits do not occur
"naturally," or at least they do not occur as a result of passivity
and indifference. They are the result of the Spirit's work within
us, the fruit of God's Spirit resulting from the ongoing work of
sanctification, but the charge remains for Timothy to participate
in this process—*pursue* these things.

   The clause encouraging Timothy to profit from the asso-
ciation with "those who call on the Lord" is not a call to
withdraw from the world. It is not a free pass on the missional
imperative.[14] Rather it is a call to benefit from the mutual
refinement of Christian community. As it flows from "flee
youthful passions," it envisions the "iron sharpening iron"
of believers (Prov. 27:17), perhaps young male believers like
those in Timothy's pastoral tribe, in covenant relationships
with each other.

   Positives today can fulfill this exhortation by seeking out
positive influences from others. Read good books, go to good
conferences, get into good pastor-study and accountability
groups, network well, collaborate well, cooperate, and consult.
Be humble enough to be in community and under authority and
not always over the community as the authority. This is doubly
important for young church planters, as they rarely have an elder
board to lead with and are prone to being foolishly independent
and impetuous.

---

[14]Lea and Griffin, *1, 2 Timothy, Titus*, 220.

14. Positively grow in discernment.

"Have nothing to do with foolish, ignorant controversies," Paul writes in verse 23. "You know that they breed quarrels." As a further development from the previous instruction to charge others not to "quarrel about words" and to personally "avoid irreverent babble," this instruction entails Timothy not just to avoid arguments or excess verbiage, but to discern the foolishness and ignorance in particular controversies. This is not redundant. It is a repeat of sorts because it is important for positives to stay on point with this for the life of the church.

When discernment deepens, an experienced positive can see these controversies coming a mile away. "You know that they breed quarrels" appeals to knowledge Timothy already has, or will at least develop an instinct for through the pastoral experience. As you grow in discernment, you can see the seeds of foolish controversies before they grow and take root. You can sniff out where these things germinate in your congregation; you can discern the personalities and the particulars that give rise to quarrels. A stubborn person may come in and hold ground on things that are no big deal. You may give him a pass on that behavior, but you keep him on your radar because you now know he's a warrior-negative, ready to die on every hill.

Discernment means you're prepared; you've got the Holy Spirit's judgment, sharpened through failure to see the landmines before you casually walk over them.

15. Positively be kind like Jesus.

Paul continues his rationale into verse 24: "And the Lord's servant must not be quarrelsome but kind to everyone." This doesn't mean that we can't be passionate people. This doesn't mean we can't take strong opinions on controversial matters, but we can't do so with a stupid and foolish argument, and we can't do it with a mean-spirited disposition. To be able to teach means not only that we are kind to those we teach, but also that we've fully researched our position on any particular issue. It means we do our homework. It means we reason and carefully think things through.

A lot of people haven't thought theological or cultural issues through very clearly, but instead revert to juvenile, knee-jerk emotionalism. They react rather than respond. Such lack of impulse control is not the mark of a positive leader, who should be thoughtful, reflective, and kind.

You need not only to have the right position. You need to reason it out in a good way with the right attitude. That's why Peter tells us to give an answer for the reason that lies within us to everyone who asks with gentleness and respect (1 Peter 3:15).

What happens in the heart of a neutral when a positive approaches any of these issues in the kindness of Jesus? A neutral often doesn't know about a lot of things that churches hold dear. But if you are simply mean-spirited or argumentative or quarrelsome with them, they're not going to learn. They're just going to become inflamed to defend their position or moved to seek out a negative to help them. This often reduces the issue to a personal debate, and the neutral will walk away not knowing who Jesus is or what the Bible says or why they should care.

This kindness extends beyond winning a neutral to cutting the loss of your neutral. It means not being resentful with people who don't see things God's way but still loving them in the grace God gives you every time you don't see things his way. You'll be very nice and kind to some people. You'll answer all of their questions to the best of your ability. You'll articulate your position graciously. And at the end they may still say, "I totally disagree. I think you're an idiot, and I don't know what you're talking about." At that point, you can't get resentful. It can't become personal. Positives do not let such situations make them bitter.

Here's the reason in the very next verse: "God may perhaps grant them repentance leading them to a knowledge of the truth." A positive wants people to meet Jesus, and so he will, like the long-suffering father in Jesus' parable, wait patiently and then run to repentant prodigals.

16. Positively harness the opportunity to teach your people.

Timothy should be "able to teach" (v. 24). There is a reason "able to teach" is a qualification for all eldership—because heretics and quarrelers and irreverent babblers are constantly teaching. Just being nice is not going to counter the cancerous spread of their impurity. You've got to be able to teach through it, preach through it, counter it vocally and vociferously. You've got to be able to point to Jesus as supreme and preeminent in all of Scripture. The gospel is "the power of God for salvation to everyone who believes" (Rom. 1:16), and God blesses the positive who lets the gospel loose in powerful proclamation. Positives build up their communities in the instruction of the Word. You protect neutrals by equipping them with the Word to withstand the rhetorical onslaught of the negatives.

17. Positively suffer patiently like Jesus.

Timothy must gird himself for the work of "patiently enduring evil" (v. 24). This conflict has apparently been ongoing for years (1 Tim. 1:3–4; 4:7). Timothy likely feels in over his head and at the end of his rope. Yet Paul, who is not shy about rebukes, desires repentance in the Spirit of the living God, who is patient with us for the same reason (2 Peter 3:9). But Paul is also willing to call a spade a spade, and he makes a theological point while doing so. He is not placating Timothy; he is not urging him to sort of let bygones be bygones. He clearly defines what Timothy must do as "endure" and what he must endure as "evil." Raymond Collins elaborates:

> The Pastor has come up with a new word to describe the kind of patience that he expects Timothy to have. Rather than use the common terminology . . . he has coined a new word, *anexikakon*, literally, "bearing evil" (*anechomai* + *kakon*). The task at hand is the correction of opponents in a kind and mild manner.[15]

In the pastoral world you will have trouble. But take heart, for Jesus, your Senior Pastor, has overcome the world. This is the gospel of suffering—when you patiently endure evil and persecution and various ministry setbacks, you are sharing in the sufferings of Christ. You are being formed in the image of Christ.

A positive doesn't immediately grumble under the weight of suffering as if he is owed an easy life. He does not claim his rights because as a servant he has none. He praises the name of Jesus and asks God to teach him whatever is needed in the time of discomfort. A positive accepts God's allowance of evil just as he eagerly accepts God's giving of good.

Such work is a brilliant testimony to the sovereignty of God and the gospel of suffering, especially to the neutrals who need to witness the positives "filling up what is lacking in Christ's afflictions" (Col. 1:24).

We see the positive charge of a neutral in defense against the negative perhaps most clearly here, in the challenging of evil

---

[15]Raymond F. Collins, *1 & 2 Timothy and Titus: A Commentary* (Louisville, KY: Westminster, 2002), 242.

with patient goodness. A positive leader, patiently enduring evil in such a way, may find that a neutral might eventually see, with Joseph's eyes, that what a negative meant for evil, God meant for good (Gen. 50:20).

18. Positively correct gently.

Paul wants Timothy to be "correcting his opponents with gentleness" (v. 25). Why with gentleness? Because positives want the gospel to win. They are not trying to win. They want the gospel to win—and not merely for the sake of the negatives who may or may not be won to Jesus, but for the sake of the neutrals who already are. When you correct heretics or discord-spreaders with gentleness, you minister well to the naïve and impressionable believers looking on. It is possible that, here in verse 25, Paul actually has the embattled neutrals in mind. Fee writes,

> The greater difficulty is with the word translated *opponents*, an extremely rare word that can refer either to the *opponents* themselves or to "those who are adversely affected" (Bernard) by the opponents. Is Timothy to discipline his opponents, as 1 Timothy 1:20 might allow? Or is he to correct or re-educate those who have been "taken in" by the false teachers? This is not easy to determine, since both are elsewhere seen as entrapped by Satan. . . . It is probably safe to say that it at least includes the people who have been so ensnared. . . .[16]

As a negative scratches a neutral's itching ear, it will do little good to come up and slap the neutral in the face. But we cannot ignore the need for correction. While we must rebuke when rebuke is called for, positives must remember that the goal is not to slap some sense into the naïve, but to pull them toward safety, gently but firmly. In general, a positive makes sure his words are

---

[16]Fee, *1 and 2 Timothy, Titus*, 215.

tender and seasoned with salt (Col. 4:6) because he may have to
eat them tomorrow.

19. Positively desire good for your enemies.

In 2 Timothy 2:25–26, Paul writes, "God may perhaps grant
them repentance leading to a knowledge of the truth, and they
may come to their senses and escape from the snare of the devil,
after being captured by him to do his will."

Positively desiring the good of your enemies is the way of
Jesus. We do not battle against flesh and blood, so it makes no
sense to pastor through these situations as if our opponents are
anything more than pawns of our true enemy or as if the negative circumstances we find ourselves in are personal when they
are in truth providential, meant for our good and the increase of
our wisdom. We do this by loving our enemies and blessing those
who persecute us.

Let us hone in on Paul's curious use of "come to their
senses." It would behoove us to remember that the unrepentant
are in bondage to their sin. We must preach hard against sin
but gently against people, particularly neutrals who have not
"come to their senses" as the prodigal son did only after he had
hit rock bottom (Luke 15:17). They may never repent. But then
again, God may grant them repentance. And therein lies another
important theological point—we will not bludgeon anyone into
repentance with argumentative skill or any amount of pastoral
maneuvering. We may be used of God, but it is God who grants
repentance. The work of positive pastoral ministry trusts God for
the results and hopes for repentance of all who appear hardened.

Church discipline is exactly that—discipline. It is only transi-
tory punishment. It is not meant to destroy anyone. So when a
positive must regretfully work to discipline those in his church,

he always does so with restoration in mind, with the glory of gospel reconciliation held out as the ultimate goal. He does not seek to demoralize his opponents but seeks to wake them up to their sin. Tough love can be a severe mercy, but positives do not use such knowledge as an excuse to beat up their enemies.

20. Positively use your energy to win converts, not arguments.

If we had to put one overarching mark of positive ministry on the entire passage, it would be this—gospel-fruit is our "win." We must positively minister in order to win the lost, not to win personal fame, intellectual credibility, job security, or any other measure of success. Jesus came to seek and save what is lost; we are not above adopting this mission as our own. It is the missional imperative. There are lots of young pastors talking shop in gathering places real and virtual, and that's all it ends up being—shoptalk. Missional theory displaces missional practice. It is not a mark of positive ministry to talk a good game, to even beat all your Christian opponents with an able defense of missional evangelism and innovative ministry and strong ecclesiology so long as the lost wander around outside untouched by any of it.

Leaders, where is your energy directed? Where is your time dedicated? What consumes your mind? What keeps you up late at night? Be careful that you do not drift into idolatry, even idolatry that looks like successful ministry.

In 2 Timothy 4:5–7, Paul writes,

> As for you, always be sober-minded, endure suffering, do the work of an evangelist, fulfill your ministry. For I am already being poured out as a drink offering, and the time of my departure has come. I have fought the good fight, I have finished the race, I have kept the faith.

That's the win. That's the end game. Ben Witherington writes, "If there is one underlying motif or maxim to all that is said about leadership in the Pastorals, it is that character counts, and its development and display in one's behavior are mandatory."[17] A positive is someone who wants to be humbly authentic, someone who knows it will profit him nothing to gain the world but lose his soul.

The most positive action you can take is to check your ego at the door—or better yet, nail it to the cross—and honorably, gently, passionately, zealously, wisely, and patiently minister the gospel in word and deed for the sake of a dying world in need of Jesus.

---

[17]Ben Witherington III, *Letters and Homilies for Hellenized Christians, Volume 1: A Socio-Rhetorical Commentary on Titus, 1–2 Timothy, and 1–3 John* (Downers Grove, IL: InterVarsity, 2006), 341.

4

SHADOWLANDS: PITFALLS AND PARODIES OF GOSPEL-CENTERED MINISTRY

(2 Timothy 3:1–9)

K. Edward Copeland

WHAT MATTERS MOST

My friend was fighting for every breath. He had called me to his room in the intensive care unit to help draft his last will and testament. He told me that the books in his extensive theological library, amassed over half a century of pastoral ministry, were to be divided equally between a select group of young preachers. His estate was to be equally divided among his children. His ultimate concern, however, was less legal and more theological; the legacy he was most concerned about was not the type that can be disposed of via the probate process.

Struggling to get comfortable as air was forcefully pumped into his lungs through a BiPAP ventilator he inched closer to the edge of the bed nearest my seat. I tried to lean in to hear his last and secret desires. With uncharacteristic uncertainty he whispered, "Who will succeed me? Who can I trust to hold the line of truth?" He went on to bemoan the fact that there is a generation of preachers who are looking for glory where Christ promised tribulation. "They want big things and big names. But they don't know how to handle the truth."

When Paul told Timothy what I am about to tell you,

Timothy was not at Paul's bedside. Paul was not whispering; he was writing. But the urgency of this text is familiar to me in a personal and palpable way. When you know your time is short, you don't focus on trivial matters.

TIME IS WINDING DOWN

In this brief letter Paul has been talking to his diffident protégé about how to conduct his ministry of the gospel faithfully. He has admonished Timothy to follow his pattern of steadfastness. He has encouraged him to avoid the contaminating influence of false doctrine and to handle the truth truthfully. He has charged him to be positive even in negative circumstances and with negative people.

This paragraph is structured as a thematic funnel. It starts out with a general statement in the form of a command. Paul commands Timothy to recognize a simple fact—the tone of the final chapter of time will be onerous. Next he describes the character of the people who will make that season so difficult to bear and commands Timothy to avoid such people. Then he turns to a specific subset of that group who are especially pernicious and calls out their modus operandi and the profile of their usual victims. Finally he references a specific biblical example of that insidious group and makes a pointed statement about their inevitable comeuppance. In doing so he opens up a main artery of the good news that ought to ever give us hope.

Another way to look at the structure of the text is to pay attention to the present imperatives. In verse 1 Paul says that Timothy needs to know something. Then at the end of verse 5 as he is about to turn a corner, he tells Timothy that he needs to avoid certain people. The first imperative suggests that the gospel minister ought to be aware, intimately and progressively, that in the last days there will be difficult, fierce, and troublesome times. Because of that the faithful gospel-minister must, according to the second imperative, purposefully avoid and completely turn away from gospel-impersonators.

The word translated "last" is the same word in the Greek that forms the basis for the English word "eschatology." It refers to the days that constitute the final sequence in a countdown. When Paul uses the terminology "last days," he is referring to those days that started at the advent of Christ. His point of reference is God's time clock. According to God's timetable, once Jesus invaded this planet the fourth quarter started. Since Christ appeared we have been living in the last days. We are in the last lap. We are in the last leg of the relay. We are in the coda of history. In music theory the coda is the final section of a musical piece where typically there is more rhythmic activity and dramatic intensity. We are moving toward the climax of history.

Just as Paul's recognition that his time was short informed his conversation, our recognition of where we are in God's timetable should inform our ministry of the Word. When you do not have much time left, you tend to zero in on and highlight the things that are most important. Failure to recognize the urgency of the hour will cause you to waste time on the inconsequential.

Since we are in the last days, we have no time for recreational preaching. We have no time for preaching for response rather than results. Imagine yourself a lawyer with a client on death row. Your client is about to be executed at midnight. If it was 11:50 p.m. and you had only one last opportunity to make an appeal to the governor to secure a pardon, you would not mince words. You would not try to impress with rhetorical pyrotechnics. Theologically speaking it is 11:50 p.m. Christ is due back momentarily. The pardon has been granted, but the inmates have not heard. If they do not hear about and accept the pardon in time, they will spend eternity in hell.

TROUBLESOME PEOPLE, DIFFICULT DAYS

According to the text the last days will include seasons that will be difficult, troublesome, and hard to bear. The only other place the word translated "difficult" is used in the New Testament is in Matthew 8:28, where Jesus encountered those two demonized men in the country of the Gadarenes. Though most translations render the word "difficult" or "troublesome," I believe the connotation in this context has as its underpinning the tone of violence. The times will be fierce, violent. Why? Not because of famine, disease, or natural disasters but because of the people who populate that time.

Paul points out that there will be a certain type of people who make the times so difficult, and he goes on to provide a list of their characteristics. The list is not exhaustive but indicative. It represents the pathology of a community, society, culture, a country gone awry. Many competent commentators have done exhaustive work on unpacking and grouping the characteristics on this list. I would like to focus on the real problem that this list points to.

The real problem is Copernican in essence. As you may remember from high school science class, before the Polish astronomer Nicolaus Copernicus came along, scientists believed in the geocentric model of the solar system. They thought every-thing revolved around the earth. Copernicus proposed a model of the solar system whereby the planets orbited around the sun.

What Paul is pointing out is that in the last days there will be a wholesale fundamental shift in our perception of the nature of reality. A reverse Copernican revolution will take place. In the last days the center of all existence will be self instead of God. Life centered on self creates a black hole of degradation. In the black hole of self-centeredness, all types of sin and rebellion will brew. When the Son is no longer the center and self becomes the center, then people will be lovers of self, lovers of money, boastful, arrogant, blasphemous, disobedient to parents, etc. You can add on to Paul's list. The root of the problem is this inherent tendency in humanity to try to re-create reality so that we are the center.

This root issue manifests itself in misdirected love. Instead of people loving God as God, they will love self to the point of deification. Because they love self, they will do anything and everything to gratify self. This misdirected love expresses itself in misdirected energies. People will pursue things that are good as if they were ultimate. Idolatry is the chief expression of that effort—making and remaking gods in our image.

The only true God says, "You shall be holy for I am holy."

When self becomes the center, then we try to remake God and reorder his nature. "You (God) shall be (in my mind) _____, for I am _____." You shall be greedy, for I am greedy. You shall be vindictive, for I am vindictive.

THE TRUE SOURCE OF OUR POWER

In verse 5 Paul indicates that the tragedy of this wholesale self-centeredness is that it will not be confined to the secular world. The real problem with this vortex of ungodliness is that those who profess to be the people of God will be the ones displaying these characteristics. If the difficult nature of the last days was relegated just to the fact that people who propound atheism acted in certain ways, that would be one thing. But the problem is that there will be some professing Christians who are practical atheists. They will give lip-service but not life-service. They will say that they are one thing, but their fruit does not bear witness. They will have a form, but will deny the power that form would indicate they have—barren fig trees, paintings of bread, wells without water, clouds without rain. "Timothy, make sure that you don't overemphasize the external to the extent that you miss the fact that it is really about the internal." That is Paul's warning.

In the last days religion will prosper, but so will wickedness, because what will pass for religion won't have any dynamite in it. Holding to a form of religion but denying its dynamite. Young preacher, always be mindful that you can arrange the wood, but only God can send the fire. The power is not in your external practices. The power is not in your performance. Sometimes we act like that neurotic rooster who thought the sun was coming up because he was crowing. Somehow we think the ministry is being effective because of what we do. If you are sitting on a plane and you feel that the plane is not going fast enough, flapping your arms will not make the plane go faster. Some of us in ministry think that our little flailing about is going to make it be more effective. There is only one Pilot. He has the wheel. He has the map and the throttle. He determines where we are going and how soon we will get there. Stop flapping.

Power is not in performance. Power is not in passion. Just raising the voice doesn't insure power. Just because it is emotive does not mean it has dynamite. Power and passion are not necessarily synonymous. Remember Elijah's encounter with God? God was not in the wind, the earthquake, or the fire. He spoke through a still, small voice. Because it is sensational does not necessarily mean that God is in it.

Where is the power? Read Romans 1:16. "For I am not

ashamed of the gospel, for it is the power of God for salvation to everyone who believes, to the Jew first and also to the Greek."[1] Dynamite is inherent in the message. The gospel is dynamite. It has resident power to change things. Read 1 Corinthians 1:18. "For the word of the cross is foolishness to those who are perishing, but to us who are being saved it is the power of God." It is the message of the cross that has the dynamite to transform men's lives. But don't forget Acts 1:8: "But you will receive power when the Holy Spirit has come upon you; and you shall be My witnesses both in Jerusalem, and in all Judea and Samaria, and even to the remotest part of the earth." It is the Word of God energized by the Holy Spirit of God that brings about transformation. It is not about your performance, passion, or even your proficiency in godly disciplines that ultimately makes the difference. It is all about God.

GET THE FACTS STRAIGHT

In these last days some of us have mistakenly majored on form rather than the power that form would suggest is present. In the last days there will be a subset of these self-centered people who will focus on religiosity rather than relationship, the external rather than internal, form rather than power.

Paul says avoid, turn away from, purposefully have nothing to do with such men. That means personally, virtually, electronically, absolutely. You cannot afford to start picking up the habits of someone who is mimicking true gospel-ministry. Don't impersonate an impersonator. So avoid, turn off, run from anything or anybody that emphasizes presentation over praxis and form over power.

Paul then turns his attention to a subset of that subset. "For

---

[1]Unless otherwise noted, Scripture quotations in this chapter are from the NASB.

among them are those. . . ." The phenomenon he is about to describe, though arising out of a specific cultural framework, is pertinent on many levels. If the power is in the gospel-message, then it strikes me that as proclaimers or heralds of the gospel we are in one sense merely reporters. In other words, modern-day reporters function in the same way heralds did in antiquity. Both herald and reporter are supposed to accurately disseminate the facts.

A herald is someone who reports important information. The best heralds were those who were eyewitnesses. Sometimes if you are not an eyewitness you might get the message wrong or report the facts incompletely. You will recall that incident in 2 Samuel 18 where Joab and his men were putting down Absalom's rebellion. Absalom was killed and someone needed to go report about the death of the king's son. A man named Ahimaaz, the son of Zadok, asked permission to run and report the news. Joab refused to allow him and instead commissioned a Cushite to run and tell what he had seen. Ahimaaz ran anyway and outran the appointed messenger. When Ahimaaz got to where he was supposed to report the news, he did not have the full story. David asked about his son, but the best Ahimaaz could say was that "I saw a great tumult but I did not know what it was" (v. 29). He became a useless herald because he did not have accurate information regarding the death of the king's son.

I point that out because as we turn our attention to examine a parody of true gospel-centered ministry, there are some interesting links between heralds, reporters, and preachers. Heralds reported the facts. They disseminated the news. They did not add anything or take anything away.

The power of the gospel is found in the truth of the verifiable facts that form the basis of the message. "For I delivered to you as of first importance what I also received, that Christ died for our sins according to the Scriptures, and that He was buried, and that He was raised on the third day according to the Scriptures, and that He appeared to Cephas, then to the twelve" (1 Cor. 15:3–5). Christ died for our sins, he was buried, and he was raised on the third day. These are facts that formulate the basis of the gospel.

Paul is arguing that we need to guard against allowing in the church among preachers what has happened in secular society among reporters. In modern American culture, we no longer celebrate journalists and objective journalism in the classic sense. We celebrate political/social/cultural commentators and sensationalism posing as reporting. We have people giving opinions about what they think the news is. We have television personalities posing as reporters who twist, spin, interpret, and omit facts to further their own ideological agendas. As tragic as that is, what is more damnable is that we have some pulpiteers posing as preachers who are not actually proclaiming news about the King's Son. Instead they are giving their opinions about social, political, and cultural matters and drawing large crowds in the process but offering no good news in the truest sense.

Paul says we need to watch out because in the last days there will be a subset of the group of self-centered deniers of the power of the gospel who are especially devious. "Among them are those. . . ." They creep into homes. They surreptitiously infiltrate households and captivate weak women. These particular "creeps" specialize in appealing to and approaching those who have a lot of time on their hands. Paul is not arguing that women are inherently spiritually weaker than men. That is not the issue at hand in Paul's statement. Paul had already prophesied in Acts 20 that in Ephesus there would be people who would rise up within the church and draw away disciples after them by twisting the truth. There would also be "savage wolves" from the outside that would infiltrate the congregation. The point is that these false teachers would prey on the most vulnerable. In this context it happened to be women who opened their homes to these charlatans.

Paul describes their victims as weak-willed or frivolous women. "Little women" is the literal translation. These women are described as such because they are laden with, heaped up with, and burdened down with sins and led away by various ungodly impulses. But the crux of their problem is in verse 7 as captured in the phrase "always learning and never able to come to the knowledge of the truth." In other words, they are ever enrolling in spiritual classes but never graduating to repentance, ever learning but never matriculating into application. These people mistakenly thought that exposure was the same thing as experience. Like many today, they thought that because they heard it or had been around it that somehow they had mastered it.

In these last days we live in a society that is oversaturated with information. We have information that we cannot assimilate or apply. On a daily basis most of us hear and see reports and images on the wars in Iraq and Afghanistan. Yet most of us would be hard-pressed to explain the difference between Al Qaeda and the Taliban. We do not understand and cannot express what is happening with the Shiites and the Sunnis. We hear the talking heads on television report incessantly on the ups and downs of the economy. Yet we cannot accurately define a derivative or a junk bond. We hear it every day but we don't what it actually means.

In the last days the Bible says we will be overfed but undernourished as it relates to spiritual matters. We will have spiritual color commentators preaching recreationally and primarily appealing to those who are burdened down with sins and driven by sinful impulses. Their victims will have just enough truth to be inoculated against the Truth. They will hear just enough "gospel" to hinder them from receiving the true gospel of Jesus Christ. They will be immunized against the gospel by a false expression of religion given as a placebo for their frail consciences.

TIME-LIMITED OPPOSITION

Paul goes on to point out two specific examples of this type of opposition to God's program in the persons of Jannes and Jambres. These names are not mentioned in the Old Testament, but have been passed down through tradition as the purported names of the two Egyptian magicians that opposed Moses. As Moses threw down his staff, turning it into a snake, they threw down theirs and performed the identical miracle. They went on to duplicate Moses' signs but only up to a point.

Paul says that in the last days false teachers will oppose the truth just like Jannes and Jambres opposed Moses. It is interesting that Paul was not afraid to call names. In every chapter of this book Paul gives the name of at least two people that Timothy needs to watch out for. In chapter 1 it was Phygelus and Hermogenes. In chapter 2 it was Hymenaeus and Philetus. In chapter 4 it will be Demas and Alexander. The point is that in every age there will be those who oppose the truth and reject the faith, but because they want a following, they will put on a tremendous impersonation of true gospel-ministry. Their parodies will be variegated and multi-flavored but predictable nonetheless because there is nothing new under the sun.

Paul points out that just as Jannes and Jambres opposed

Moses, the same type of men will oppose Timothy's message. He emphasizes it so that Timothy will not be caught off guard and suppose that everyone is going to like him because he is a preacher. You need to be on guard so that you will not only be able to identify the idols in your culture and your community but also the impersonators of gospel-ministry.

The good news is in verse 9. They will not make further progress "for their folly will be obvious to all." Paul is saying that Jannes and Jambres in every age pose a very real threat but have a very real, God-ordained limit. In the last days things will get progressively worse. God promises that. They will get worse not merely because of natural disasters even though those will intensify. They will get worse primarily because of the people who populate these last days. Among the people populating the last days will be a group who profess to be believers but in fact are impersonators. Out of that group there will be a subset of imposters who will occupy pulpits but have no power. But young man, do not get upset, because ultimately their folly will be exposed.

The bottom line is God is still in control. The good news is that God is not worried about it, and never should you be. The real threat has a real limit and a set time for self-destruction. We do not live in a dualistic universe. It is not that good and evil are evenly matched and we do not know who is going to win. This is not a contest between opponents who have parity of power. God controls this universe. In God's own time and according to God's timetable all evil will be eradicated. One day even death will have a funeral.

This text lets us know that God puts a limit on foolishness. Every lie has an expiration date, but truth will march on from everlasting to everlasting. Even though evil is temporarily successful, it will ultimately be swallowed up in utter humiliation. Evil's foolishness will be exposed for what it is.

This word "folly" is used only one other place in the New Testament. In Luke 6:11 it is translated "filled with rage" (NASB), "filled with madness" (KJV), or "furious" (NIV). It has the connotation of being so enraged that you are senseless, so upset that you cannot think through what is going on. In Luke 6 after Jesus healed a man, his opponents were so enraged that they started plotting our Savior's death. That folly ultimately led them to bring trumped-up charges and railroad Jesus through several kangaroo courts and convict him. In their folly they did not realize something that this text reiterates and we must never forget. God is so awesome that he can take the foolishness of evil men and let it redound to his glory. That is what the cross is about. "Which none of the princes of this world knew: for had they known it, they would not have crucified the Lord of glory" (1 Cor. 2:8 KJV). In their folly and foolishness, they crucified our Lord, not realizing that by doing so they were activating the very means by which he would be crowned Victor. He is the unified, title-wearing champion of the universe, having conquered death, hell, and the grave.

WE WIN

If you are a proclaimer of the gospel, you are on the winning side. Act like it. Why are you so distressed about who is in office? God is on the throne, and he is not up for reelection. Why are you so distressed about the lies propagated by evil men when you have the truth? Preach the truth. That's where the power to make a difference is. If you allow the Holy Spirit to empower your ministry of the Word and you allow him to energize not just your preaching and teaching but your living and your loving, then what difference does it make what evil men are doing? That does not mean that we do not confront evil. It does not mean that we don't stand against error. It does mean that we should not act like we are orphans. We have a Father who knows exactly what's going on, and he has the power to do something about whatever is not right.

Be faithful in your proclamation, knowing that it is neither your performance nor your passion that is making the difference. It is the power of the Holy Spirit and the truth of the facts that you are accurately reporting. So get the facts straight. Stop preaching for response. Preach for results.

They say that J. S. Bach died writing a fugue. It was not complete. Years later as the fugue was analyzed, musicians discovered that Bach put his name in the musical notation of the piece. In German musical notation, B-natural is notated as what they would consider an "h." So he put B-A-C-H throughout the fugue in the most moving sections. It was not until long after his death that people recognized that if you play the fugue correctly then his name rings through every page. His name is living on in his music because he wrote into the very fabric of this masterpiece—BACH.

The good news is that we have a composer who wrote his name in every line of history. Our plight is to play our notes correctly. If we follow his notations correctly, his name will sing even in the folly of evil men. He wrote even the disharmony of rebellion into the melody of this magnum opus. The song is "God wins."

I've become shamefully addicted to a television show entitled *24*. Every Monday I tune in to watch the exploits of Agent Jack Bauer as he tries to save the world. I got addicted several seasons ago when during one Christmas break my wife and I watched the first few seasons on DVD. I would stay up to the wee hours of the night trying to see how Jack would get out of the next impossible situation. In one episode during those early seasons, Jack actually died. It was very late at night when I was watching this episode, so it presented me with a dilemma. Should I lose sleep to try to see how Jack was going to work this out, or should I try to go to bed knowing that the suspense would not allow me to rest well anyway? As I was debating about what I should do, I happened to notice the credits at the end of the presentation. Until that time I had not noticed that Keifer Sutherland, the actor who plays the character Jack Bauer, was the executive producer of the show. Once I saw that I turned off the television and went straight to sleep. I realized that as long as the executive producer of the story is also its main character, that character will always come out on top even through death.

In the final chapter of God's masterpiece called time, don't stay up at night wondering how it's going to come out. The good news is our Executive Producer has secured our victory. He is the main character of history. According to the script, one day every knee will bow and every tongue will confess this truth.

Do your work. Do it well. But do not stay up nights wondering how it will turn out. We win.

5

PREACH THE WORD!

(2 Timothy 3:10–4:5)

Bryan Chapell

In a recent letter to supporters, China mission leader Sam Ling wrote, "The church in China is feeling the impact of neo-evangelicalism and post-conservatism. . . . Overseas Chinese seminaries are evolving into post-conservative schools. The church is losing her orthodoxy. . . . We must call the church to faithful adherence to . . . the inspiration and inerrancy of Scripture." These are amazing words. Within two generations of the explosion of Christianity in China that we have all applauded, there is now an erosion of confidence in the truth of Scripture. We should not be amazed at such a thing. This is not a new problem.

In 2 Timothy 3:10–4:5, for example, the apostle Paul writes to his protégé Timothy—in the *same* generation that the gospel came to Ephesus—to exhort the young preacher to continue teaching that the Bible *must* be believed. False teachers have already crept into the church, eroding confidence in the Scriptures. This early reality reminds us that *every* generation—regardless of the orthodoxy preceding it—must determine anew the answer to the question, "Will we believe the Bible?"

To answer this question for our own time, we should consider again Paul's focus on this issue in 3:16–17. To discern the full import of these verses, however, we will also need to consider key ideas in surrounding verses. Our understanding will grow as we read the full text, remembering that Paul has just warned Timothy about what false teachers say and do before the apostle writes this:

> *You, however, have followed my teaching, my conduct, my aim in life, my faith, my patience, my love, my steadfastness, my persecutions and sufferings that happened to me at Antioch, at Iconium, and at Lystra—which persecutions I endured; yet from them all the Lord rescued me. Indeed, all who desire to live a godly life in Christ Jesus will be persecuted, while evil people and impostors will go on from bad to worse, deceiving and being deceived. But as for you, continue in what you have learned and have firmly believed, knowing from whom you learned it and how from childhood you have been acquainted with the sacred writings, which are able to make you wise for salvation through faith in Christ Jesus. All Scripture is breathed out by God and profitable for teaching, for reproof, for correction, and for training in righteousness, that the man of God may be competent, equipped for every good work.*
>
> *I charge you in the presence of God and of Christ Jesus, who is to judge the living and the dead, and by his appearing and his kingdom: preach the word; be ready in season and out of season; reprove, rebuke, and exhort, with complete patience and teaching. For the time is coming when people will not endure sound teaching, but having itching ears they will accumulate for themselves teachers to suit their own passions, and will turn away from listening to the truth and wander off into myths. As for you, always be soberminded, endure suffering, do the work of an evangelist, fulfill your ministry. (2 Tim. 3:10–4:5)*

Los Angeles was burning on the evening of the first Rodney King verdict. Many of us remember why. During an arrest, a video camera had recorded white policemen beating King, an African-American, and those officers had just been exonerated. The predominantly black neighborhoods of South Central Los Angeles exploded in retaliation and riot. The rage was vengeful, violent, and indiscriminate. News cameras filmed a group of young men dragging a Hispanic worker from his truck, knocking him to the ground, and brutally beating him.

Into that angry mob waded an elderly, black minister named Bennie Newton, whose name will forever bring honor to the office of pastor. Risking his own life, Pastor Newton repeatedly stepped in the way of those who were delivering the blows. He took the punches and kicks on his own back and legs. He shouted above the curses of the attackers, "This man has done nothing wrong! You must stop this. You must stop this!" And eventually they did stop. They turned away in disgust from an old man who had faced their fury with nothing more than a Bible in his hands.

Why did he have a Bible? Surely it was a symbol of his office, but it was also a statement of his faith that whether facing life or death, he would entrust himself—body and soul—to what this book attests. Why bank so much on a book? We have to answer that question because *what we believe about this book will determine what we say and do to safeguard those whom God puts in our care.* If there is erosion of faith in this generation, it will be because we who are church leaders forget the nature of *the book.* Forgetting the nature of the book is so easy to do. This reminding letter in the first generation of the gospel of Christ makes clear our tendency to forget the nature of God's Word. And, so that we will not forget, the apostle Paul reminds us in this letter to Timothy of the nature of the Scriptures. He tells us that in them we *hear the voice of God, see the hand of God, and know the heart of God.*

HEARING THE VOICE OF GOD

Hearing the voice of God requires a foundation of belief in what the Bible says about itself. Paul says in our passage that the

Bible is "breathed out by God" (v. 16). These words translate
the Greek term *theopneustos*, which means "God-breathed."
In theological circles we refer to this as the doctrine of biblical
inspiration.

The Meaning of Inspiration

A few years ago, an accreditation team came to Covenant
Theological Seminary, where I am president, to examine us for
the renewal of our license to operate. The head of the accreditation team was the dean at a major Midwestern university. He met
with me early in the visit and asked me to identify some of the
distinctions of our school. I said to him, "One of the key commitments we have is that the Bible is inspired." "That's great,"
he said, "I think the Bible is inspiring, too." I had to smile and
say, "That's not exactly what I mean."

What *do* we mean when we say that the Bible is inspired?
The Greek term actually refers to "expiration," breath being
breathed out as one speaks. When you speak, you feel your
breath come out as the words are expressed. So Paul contends
that when Scripture was written, God was breathing out his
Word. Just as God breathed life into humanity at creation, so,
Paul says, God breathes spiritual life into the Scriptures so that
we could be a new creation.

Exactly how men could write words that reflect their situations and personalities and yet still be God's Word to us is a
mystery. We don't understand it entirely, but elsewhere Scripture
describes the process. The apostle Peter writes, "No prophecy of
Scripture comes from someone's own interpretation. . . . but men
spoke from God as they were carried along by the Holy Spirit"
(2 Peter 1:20–21). Paul states the consequence of this process
when he commends believers at Thessalonica for receiving his

message "not as the word of men but as what it really is, the word of God" (1 Thess. 2:13).

Augustine summarizes well the import of these truths by saying simply, "Where the Bible speaks, God speaks."

The Significance of Inspiration

Because it is God-breathed, Scripture is God's very Word to us. This is not just an abstract observation for academic discussion; it is one of the most precious truths Christians possess to survive and thrive every day.

IMPLICATIONS

In everyday life and in the greatest trials of my life, God speaks to me in his Word. When I believe what the Bible says about itself, I have the privilege of hearing God's voice. At a young people's meeting, a fresh-out-of-seminary youth pastor I know attempted to impress his group with the wonder of the divine inspiration of Scripture. He gathered the teens in a circle, put a chair in the middle, and handed out Bible verses printed on cards to everyone in the circle. The person sitting in the middle chair was blindfolded and asked to tell the group some problem he or she was experiencing. Then, someone in the circle was supposed to read an applicable Bible verse that dealt with the problem. The idea was that because the person in the middle chair was blindfolded, he or she would perceive the verse being read as though God himself was speaking through the words of Scripture.

The youth leader thought this was a pretty clever idea. The kids thought it was pretty dumb. None of them would talk about a problem more significant than how to get an A on Mrs. Bailey's math quizzes—and there really wasn't a good Bible verse for that. The whole thing was going miserably, and giggles rather than the voice of God predominated.

Then a new girl who had been sitting on the periphery volunteered to sit in the middle chair. The giggling subsided a bit as she was blindfolded because no one knew her well enough to know how she would react. Then she spoke, "I am so miserable. I don't know if I can stand my life anymore." No one knew what to say or do, and most just looked down in embarrassment. But one boy looking down saw the verse in his hand and read, "God is faithful; he will not let you be tempted beyond what you can bear. But when you are tempted, he will also provide a way out so that you can stand up under it" (1 Cor. 10:13, NIV).

"No one cares for me," said the girl. But then another girl in the outer circle read, "I have loved you with an everlasting love; I have drawn you with loving-kindness" (Jer. 31:3, NIV).

"You don't understand," said the girl in the blindfold with a voice now desperate, "my parents kicked me out last night and said, 'Never come back!'" Then someone read, "I will never leave you nor forsake you" (Josh. 1:5, NIV). They took the blindfold off the girl. She was crying, and through her tears she asked a question, "Why doesn't God *really* talk to me that way?" Said the youth pastor, "He just did. Because the Bible is inspired, it is God's very Word. God *did* speak to you with those verses."

Even those of us who are much more mature in our faith can be so silly about what we think we want from God. We think that life would be so much easier if God would just miraculously write his will in the clouds or speak in the thunder. But if he wrote in the clouds, then the words would all blow away, and if he spoke in the thunder, then his voice would fade away. So instead God says in essence, "Would you mind if I just wrote my words down for you, so that you could have them wherever you go and whenever they are needed." Inspired Scripture is the greater miracle. God has given us his abiding Word so that we are not without his voice in all the trials and temptations of this life. In the Bible, we proclaim, God yet speaks to his people.

The leaders of the Reformation expressed these truths with particular power. Martin Luther said, "The church is God's mouth house." When the Bible is proclaimed in the church, God is yet speaking through the church to his people and to the world. We can alter an old children's rhyme to express this truth simply:

Here's the church. Here's the steeple.
Open the Word. God speaks to his people.

In the Second Helvetic Confession the Swiss Reformers made this point in very strong terms: "The preaching of the Word of God, is the Word of God." To the extent that our preaching is true to Scripture, God's words yet echo in the church. His voice is available to his people—even when it comes through our human mouths—when we are faithful in preaching his Word.

John Calvin expressed the truth of inspiration in words so strong that were it not Calvin who spoke, we might question if such things should be said. He said, "God has chosen so to anoint the lips and tongues of his servants that, when they speak, the voice of Jesus yet resounds in them."

We are accustomed in Reformed circles to thinking that Christ is the ultimate audience of all we preach. We are less accustomed to thinking that Jesus is the *speaker* as well as the audience. When our words are true to his Word, Jesus yet comes and ministers to his people in the preaching of the Word. The human instrument is used, but Jesus speaks. That little plaque that appears in so many churches behind the pulpit for only the preacher to see ("Sir, we would see Jesus.") could well be altered to say, "Sir, we would hear Jesus." God's voice is present to his people when we speak the truth of his Word in the pulpit, in Sunday school, in the counseling office, or in a child's bedroom. However great are the challenges we face, we have this great comfort in preaching God's Word—we are not alone. By his Word and Spirit, Jesus is with us and in us, speaking to his people as we proclaim what the Bible says.

What I am contending—because the Scriptures attest the same—is that when we speak the truths of the Word of God, we are not simply speaking *about* Jesus, nor are we simply speaking *for* Jesus. We are speaking *as* Jesus.

EXPECTATIONS

Because Jesus speaks to his people as we speak the truth of his Word, there are expectations that naturally follow:

1. *Purity.* Since we are speaking as Jesus, we should commend his words in how we conduct ourselves. We are speaking as though God is "making his appeal through us" (2 Cor. 5:20). So, as those who speak with Christ's voice, it is legitimate to ask, "What would Jesus do?" Paul answers that question for Timothy in preceding verses: "You . . . have followed my teaching, my conduct, my aim in life, my faith, my patience, my love, my steadfastness. . . . continue in what you have learned" (2 Tim. 3:10, 14). Paul reminds Timothy that he is to "desire to live a godly life in Christ Jesus" (v. 12) and that he is called to be a "man of God" (v. 17).

The quality of our lives does not make the Word of God true or endue it with power. The Word is inherently true and powerful, but by our lives we can either add static to what God is communicating or provide clear channel. We should not let present, legitimate demands for authenticity and transparency convince us that the call to godliness is old fashioned or ineffective. In preaching the Bible, we who have the Word of Christ in our mouths are charged to commend it with the purity of our speech, habits, and motives. Do not let anyone convince you that the people of God do not desire godliness from their leaders. Piety is not passé. While no one wants sanctimonious religiosity, God's people need to know that the gospel is real and frees us from our sin. The leaders of God's people communicate the hope of the gospel by speaking and living so as to honor the Jesus we voice.

2. *Persecution.* If we speak as Jesus, we should expect that we will experience what he did—persecution. Paul appropriately warns Timothy, "You, however, have followed my teaching . . . my persecutions and sufferings that happened to me at Antioch, at Iconium, and at Lystra" (vv. 10, 11). These were the cities of riots and rocks, where crowds were stirred up against Paul and stoned him. Now Paul says, "Indeed, all who desire to live a godly life in Christ Jesus will be persecuted" (v. 12).

Many of us still sing an old hymn containing these words about the path of suffering: "It is the way the Master went, should not the servant tread it still?" If Christ experienced persecution when he spoke for God, we should not be surprised that we would experience the same when we speak for him. From outside the church and inside the church, attack will come against those who speak Jesus' words. I say this not to frighten but to forearm. When you face persecution for faithfulness, do not presume that you have done something wrong or that your situation is strange. All who are faithful will face challenges. You are not alone in suffering. You have not failed because you face pressures. "Indeed, all who desire to live a godly life in Christ Jesus will be persecuted."

3. *Power.* With wonderful pastoral wisdom Paul follows this

warning about persecution with a promise of power. We are not alone *in* suffering for God's Word, and we are not alone *when* suffering for God's Word. Paul says to Timothy, "I charge you *in the presence* of God and of Christ Jesus, who is to judge the living and the dead, and by his appearing and his kingdom: preach the word" (4:1–2).

We should be able to read this verse with new understanding when we recognize that Christ is present in the preaching of his Word. The reason that Paul can charge Timothy to faithful proclamation of the Word in the presence of God and Christ Jesus is not simply because they superintend all human activity from some heavenly perch, but because they are present in the Word preached. The presence of the living Lord stimulates a second key thought—if Christ is present, then it must be with resurrection power. Though he died, Paul says Jesus will appear to judge the living and the dead. If he who has power over death itself is present in the preaching of the Word, then vast spiritual power accompanies those who preach. This does not spell an end to all trouble; it does indicate that God's Word will accomplish what he intends as it is faithfully preached (cf. Isa. 55:11).

If a U.S. military officer cannot launch an atomic weapon without orders from the president, think how powerful must be the force unleashed that requires a charge from God and Christ Jesus! Yet this is precisely the power that is at work in us when we preach God's Word. Knowledge of this power gives Paul reason to urge Timothy to "be ready in season and out of season; reprove, rebuke, and exhort, with complete patience and teaching" (2 Tim. 4:2). Because the Word of God has such great power, we can speak its truths in season and out, expecting it to perform God's purposes.

In addition, because the power is in the Word and not us,

we can say whatever needs to be said with "complete patience and teaching." Because the Word of God has power like dynamite, then like dynamite it should be handled carefully. We can afford to be patient and "complete" our teaching when we know that the power is not in our eloquence or zeal but in the Word itself. Because the Word is so powerful, we can be very bold. We can also afford to be compassionate in manner and expression because God does not need us to strong-arm or manipulate his truth so that it will convince others. We have the Word of Christ, so it is right that we express its truths with the manner of Christ—with courage when needed and with compassion when needed. In either case, we expect the power of Christ to be present because his voice is resounding in ours.

Because the voice of Jesus is present in the proclamation of the Word, we are not alone when we preach, nor are we powerless. The One who brought creation into being when he spoke yet speaks with the power to make new creatures in Christ Jesus through the faithful proclamation of his Word. What a comfort and what an encouragement to "preach the word!"

SEEING THE HAND OF GOD

When we faithfully proclaim the truths of the Bible, not only do we have the privilege of hearing God's voice, we also get to see his hand. Seeing the hand of God also requires a foundation of belief in what the Bible says about itself. The belief that needs to be affirmed can be determined by asking the question, "How much of the Word of God is inspired?" Paul's answer: "*All* Scripture is breathed out by God" (v. 16a). All that is Scripture has the same origin—it has been inspired by God. There is a necessary implication—that which has been inspired by God will reflect his character.

A great place to see God's character reflected in his Word is Psalm 19:7–9. In this passage the psalmist is describing the nature of the various aspects of God's Word. But if you did not know that the writer was describing the Word of God, what would you think was being described? Focus just on the descriptive terms to answer the question:

> The law of the LORD is **perfect**, *reviving the soul;*
> the testimony of the LORD is **sure**, *making wise the simple;*
> the precepts of the LORD are **right**, *rejoicing the heart;*
> the commandment of the LORD is **pure**, *enlightening the eyes;*
> the fear of the LORD is **clean, enduring forever;**
> the rules of the LORD are **true**, *and* **righteous altogether.** *(Ps. 19:7–9)*

Were you to consider only the adjectives, what would you think is being described? You would think *God himself* is being described. He is perfect, sure, right, pure, clean, enduring forever, true, righteous altogether, etc. That's the point. The Word of God reflects the character of God, since he inspires it. This means that the Bible is perfect, sure, right, pure, clean, enduring forever, true, and altogether righteous—and for this reason it can be entirely trusted as the hand of God to guide us where we should go and to direct what we should do.

Theologians refer to this principle of the absolute trustworthiness of God's Word as the *doctrine of biblical inerrancy.* When we say that the Bible is inerrant, we must quickly add that our interpretations of it are not without error. Elsewhere the apostle Paul will remind Timothy that he must study to be a godly workman who is "rightly handling the word of truth" (2 Tim. 2:15). We can make wrong "divisions," but this acknowledgment does not deny the inerrancy of Scripture; it simply calls us to be skilled interpreters.

Further, if God's ways are not our ways and his thoughts are above our thoughts, then we should not be surprised that there are passages that stretch our knowledge; we can make mistakes simply because we do not understand enough. But saying that we can mess up is something entirely different from saying that God's Word is mistaken. Paul says, *"All* Scripture is breathed out by God."* That means that all that God has given as his Word reflects his perfect character. Whatever truth the Bible teaches is true.

The spirit of the age, of course, challenges this doctrine of inerrancy and points to supposed contradictions or inaccuracies in the Bible. But virtually all of these can be answered by reasonable investigation from a mind that believes God has inspired Scripture. This matter of "believing investigation" needs to be emphasized. We should not think that by logic or science we can irrefutably rebut every possible objection to Scripture. While there are many sound arguments to defend the truth of Scripture, there is always the possibility that someone will come up with an argument or discovery that we haven't considered yet. At that point we do not base our doctrine of Scripture on the sufficiency of our logic, but on the faithfulness of our God. We trust him ultimately to reveal what is true not because we can prove it to be so but because he has proven *himself* to be faithful.

The great preacher Charles Spurgeon once said that anyone who would trust Scripture must be willing to be thought a fool for twenty years before science will prove him right. In general, I like and agree with this sentiment, but still we need to be wary of the assumption that reason will serve to confirm all that Scripture attests. We must not forget that logic supports our faith but is not its sole pillar. The Westminster Divines struck a good balance when they said that by its many "incomparable excellencies" the Bible "doth abundantly evidence itself to be the Word of God, yet notwithstanding our full persuasion and assurance of the infallible truth and divine authority thereof is from the inward work of the Holy Spirit bearing witness by and with the Word in our hearts" (*WCF* I.V). By Spirit-induced faith as well as by reason-driven logic we believe the Bible to be entirely true.

If this belief in the absolute truth of Scripture sounds naïve and simplistic, please recognize that it is far more logically consistent than the arguments of those who claim that the Bible is a "good book" despite its many flaws. Many of us were trained in our college years to use the "three Ls" in responding to those who said that Jesus was just a good man. We said this could not be the case because Jesus claimed to be the Son of God. If he said this knowing he was not, then he was a *liar*. If he believed he was the Son of God when he was not, then he was a *lunatic*. But if he said he was the Son of God, and he really was, then he really is the *Lord*. In light of the claims he made, Jesus could *not* have been simply a "good man."

The same logic applies to the argument that the Bible is just a good book, though a flawed one. The Bible claims to be the Word of God—more than three thousand times some form of the phrase "Thus says the Lord" appears within its pages. Either this is a colossal lie, or it is sheer lunacy, or the Bible *is* the Word of the Lord. The Bible cannot be just a "good book."

Release from the Idolatry of Self

If the Bible is not the infallible Word of God that it claims to be, then not only should the Bible have no great significance for us, but God himself disappears from us. A professor I know once responded to a student who was challenging the total truth of Scripture by taking a pair of scissors from his desk drawer. "Here," said the professor to the student, "take this pair of scissors and cut out everything that you don't think should be in the Bible. But you should recognize that by the time you are done picking and choosing what should be included, the only wisdom that you will have left is your own."

Whenever we become the judge of what the Bible should say—when our Scriptures are only our best cut-and-paste job—then we substitute our wisdom for God's. In my mind's eye, I imagined that by the time the student was done with his scissors, his Bible looked like a string of paper dolls and each doll looked like the student. Each was a reflection of the only wisdom he would allow—his own. His Bible was a creation of his self-idolatry, from which belief in God's inerrant Word has freed us.

Release from the Isolation of Self

The great sadness of having a Bible that reflects only our own wisdom is not simply the elimination of divine wisdom, but the elimination of divine presence. There will be times in all of our lives that the darkness closes in and we cry out for God. But if our Bible contains only the content of our own wisdom, then the only sound that we will hear when we call out in the darkness is an echo of our own voices. Though usually described in academic terms, inerrancy is our freedom from a suffocating aloneness—the inevitable prison of being shut up with one's own judgments as the only guiding companion in life. Without a Bible that can be trusted beyond our own wisdom, God disappears from our lives, and human opinion alone determines what is right and wrong, proper or foolish.

But God has not disappeared. To the contrary, by his Word our Lord's hand yet guides us in the darkness. The apostle says that the Word is "profitable for teaching, for reproof, for correction, and for training in righteousness" (v. 16b). Each of these words reflects Paul's understanding of the essential truth of all Scripture:

> *Teaching:* The Bible leads us in the path of truth.
> *Reproof:* The Bible knocks us from the path of error.
> *Correction:* The Bible returns us to the path of truth.
> *Training in righteousness:* The Bible directs us in the application of truth, taking us all the way down the path of God's will for godly living.

Through all of these our Lord provides his unerring hand to lead us through the darkness of our world.

Such unerring guidance is itself an indication of the gracious heart of our God. By contrast, in *The Spectral Hand* the Victorian novelist Jean Lorrain writes a gothic tale of dinner guests invited to gain spiritual guidance by human wiles. The host invites each guest to put his hand through a curtain to grasp the spirits on the other side. If the guest can grab a fleeting specter, then the spirit will speak, revealing hidden truths. Our God does something far more miraculous and caring through his Word. By the truths of the Bible, God extends *his* hand through the veil between heaven and earth to guide us every day, everywhere, in every situation we must face; and he speaks to us with a voice that does not fade (cf. 1 Peter 1:23).

KNOWING THE HEART OF GOD

When you have the voice of God to comfort and the hand of God to guide, what you really have in Scripture is the heart of God on display. As with the voice and the hand of God, knowing the heart of God also requires a foundation of belief in what the Bible says about itself. Paul tells Timothy to "continue in what you have learned and have firmly believed, knowing . . . the sacred writings, which are able to make you wise for salvation through faith in Christ Jesus" (vv. 14, 15). The Bible reveals God's heart for his people by telling them of the salvation that is provided for them through faith in Christ.

Yet these "sacred writings" to which Paul refers could be only what we know as the Old Testament, written before Christ's coming—for most of the New Testament had not yet been produced. How could these Old Testament writings make Timothy wise for salvation through faith in Christ Jesus? Obviously, one answer is that the Old Testament Scriptures contain predictions of the coming of Christ. But there is a more comprehensive answer. Paul tells Timothy that the Scriptures have been given "that the man of God may be competent, equipped for every good work" (v. 17). The word "competent" in this phrase is a translation of the Greek *artios*, which means "complete." An important implication results from understanding Paul's statement that the Scriptures are given to "complete" us—*we are incomplete apart from the provision of God.*

How are we incomplete? That has been made apparent by what God has already revealed about himself in his Word. He is perfect, sure, right, pure, clean, and altogether righteous (see again Ps. 19:7–10). At the same time, Scripture reveals something quite different about *us.* Echoing many Old Testament texts in this passage, Paul reminds us that people naturally "will not endure sound teaching, but having itching ears they will accumulate for themselves teachers to suit their own passions, and will turn away from listening to the truth and wander off into myths" (2 Tim. 4:3–4). In short, God's nature is holy, and ours is not. There is a great disparity between his nature and ours that requires his provision in order for us to be rescued from our spiritual "incompleteness."

Because the sacred writings are always revealing God's perfections and our incompleteness, they are consistently pointing us toward the necessity of faith in someone beyond ourselves to rescue us from our spiritual destitution. If we will simply ask two questions of any passage—what does this text tell me about God and what does this text tell me about humanity—we will always discover redemptive truth glimmering. All Scripture directs us toward faith in Christ, for he is the ultimate message of all the "sacred writings." Thus, when Paul tells Timothy, "Preach the word," the apostle necessarily charges the young minister to proclaim Christ (the Incarnate Word) as the aim of all he preaches.

Our work as proclaimers of Scripture is never done when we have told God's people the duty and doctrine a passage may teach. If people are left to think that they are right with God because they *do enough* or *know enough*, then they are ultimately looking to their own strength and wisdom as the source of their salvation. They must always look toward the Savior and trust in his provision even as they respond in obedience to God and thirst for knowledge of God. Surely this is why Paul tells Timothy, "Always be sober-minded, endure suffering, *do the work of an evangelist*, fulfill your ministry" (4:5). Though Timothy has a mature ministry in Ephesus, he still must proclaim the good news that is in Christ Jesus in order to fulfill his ministry.

Living Water for Thirsty Souls

How do we remain Christ-focused in all we proclaim? The answer lies in the realization that *all* Scripture is *always* revealing the voice, hand, and heart of God. *And when you have the voice, hand, and heart of God, you have Jesus.* He is "the radiance of the glory of God and the exact imprint of his nature" (Heb. 1:3). Being faithful to the full message of Scripture is presenting

Christ, for whom the human heart thirsts. And understanding that Christ is the message of *all* Scripture explains why God's people so thirst for God's Word.

Many of us cherish the words of the psalmist, "As a deer pants for flowing streams, so pants my soul for you, O God" (Ps. 42:1). We may forget how the psalmist says that thirst is satisfied: "My soul is consumed with longing for your rules at all times. . . . I open my mouth and pant, because I long for your commandments" (Ps. 119:20, 131). Why would anyone long for God's commands? Because when those commands are rightly understood as revealing the caring voice, guiding hand, and saving heart of God—leading us to understand our need and God's provision—then we thirst for what God's Word teaches.

I have never had a more powerful impression of how the human heart thirsts for the Word than when a friend explained how he came to a saving knowledge of Jesus Christ. He was an ordained minister in a church that considered the Bible only as a work of men that should be critically dissected for its occasional truths amidst its primitive religious expressions.

By mistake my friend got hooked into a tour of Israel that had him and his girlfriend traveling with a bunch of evangelical ministers and their wives. One day the tour took them to the Garden Tomb, one of the places in Israel reputed to be where Jesus was buried and rose from the dead. The ministers decided to celebrate communion at the site. Since my friend had stayed in the background for most of the tour, the others decided that now was the time for him to do his share of ministering. He was asked to conduct the communion service. He did so. But as this unbelieving minister distributed the elements representing Christ's body and blood and he said the words of Christ's promise to come again, in the place of Jesus' resurrection, my friend was struck not only with the hypocrisy of what he was doing, but with the reality of what Christ had done.

When the service was over, the other ministers continued touring the site. My friend did not. He went back to the tour bus and waited with almost frantic desperation for the others to finish their sightseeing. He says, "For the first time in my life I was thirsty for Scripture, and I felt I would die if we did not get back to the hotel as quickly as possible so that I could read my Bible." There are streams of living water in the Word that satisfy the thirsty heart with God. For this reason the apostle Paul says clearly and passionately, "Preach the word."

Preach the Word. This should be our privilege and passion, knowing that when we do so, we share the voice, the hand, and the heart of God with thirsty people. Whether they know they are thirsty or not, their hearts' cry is always, "Give me Jesus." How do we do that? Preach the Word.

When I am alone, give me Jesus. How? Preach the Word, and his voice will minister his presence.

When I am afraid, give me Jesus. How? Preach the Word, and his hand will guide my path.

And when I am defiled, give me Jesus. How? Preach the Word, and his heart will cleanse my soul.

Give me Jesus. How? *Preach the Word.*

6

FINISHING WELL

(2 Timothy 4:6–22)

J. Ligon Duncan

I have a question for you. Do you think that Paul can get to the gospel and grace in his closing comments and greetings in this little letter? Yes, he can! And we'll see that in a moment.

Meanwhile, as we come to this final exposition of 2 Timothy, I have an exhortation for you—determine and commit yourself to read, re-read, live in, and pray the Pastoral Epistles of Paul. This is so important because the Pastorals give us apostolic instruction for life and ministry. They teach us about church administration, public worship, and the qualifications for ministers, elders, and deacons. They show us how women are to be involved in the life and ministry of the church. They tell us who ought to provide for the needy and how to give spiritual counsel to aged men and women as well as to young men and women. They stress sound doctrine, and they relate that sound doctrine to living the Christian life. They demand consecrated living. They show the value of creeds and confessions. They reveal the closing activities in the life of the apostle Paul. They disclose church life at the end of the first century, but more than that, they are written for our instruction. They show us how Christian ministry is meant to be done. They show us what Christian ministry is supposed to be like. Paul expects us to pattern our ministry today on these principles. He is not just making suggestions or offering us

the vantage point of his experience. He intends for what he says
to be practiced in all churches, everywhere (1 Tim. 3:14–15; cf.
1 Cor. 7:17; 14:33, 37–38).[1]

TWO PROBLEMATIC PARADIGMS FOR MINISTRY

The apostle Paul is laying down permanent principles, patterns,
and priorities for the Christian life and ministry in the Pastoral
Epistles. One of the reasons that it is so hugely important that we
let the Pastorals influence our ministry and shape our church life
now in the twenty-first century is that two errors have bedeviled
the Western church for the past two hundred years.

The Key Is an Updated Message

The first error claims that *if the church is going to be an effective witness to the world in its own time, then its message must
change.* The premise underlying this approach is that the message
that Paul used won't work in our current setting and thus must
change if Christianity is going to be compelling.

The Key Is in Updated Methods

The second error that has also dogged the Western church for
the last two hundred years is more common among evangelicals.
It says we don't need an updated message because the message is
basically alright, but *what we do need if we're going to be really
successful, if we're really going to reach our world and our culture, are new methods.* This approach sees our methods as the
key to reaching our culture, and it assumes that our methods
neither flow from nor are essentially related to our message. In
other words, it divorces theology from methodology (or inadequately relates them).

---

[1]William Hendrickson, *Exposition of the Pastoral Epistles* (Grand Rapids, MI: Baker, 1957).

Liberalism: Our Message Must Change

Now you perhaps recognize the first error is the error of theological liberalism. Friedrich Schleiermacher in the 1790s looked around and observed how the German Reformed church was unable to reach its culture. The culture had essentially adopted the outlook of the Enlightenment and rejected Christianity. Schleiermacher, while he was at university, had the same experience himself. His father was a very devout, simple believer, but Schleiermacher came under a deep intellectual-theological duress in his personal thinking about penal substitutionary atonement and the uniqueness of Jesus Christ. He could not believe that Jesus was the only way, and he could not believe in vicarious substitutionary atonement. So he decided that unless Christianity changed its message, it would fail to capture the culture.[2]

Schleiermacher and the liberals that followed him didn't sit down in a tavern somewhere and say, "What can we do to destroy Christianity? What can we do to wipe out the church? How can we dispense with Christian orthodoxy?" Their motivation was missiological. They wanted to reach their culture, but they thought they had to change the message in order to do so. They were not merely trying to make the message accessible. They did not simply attempt to convey the old message in the language and context of their emerging culture. No, they changed the substance of the message because they believed this to be necessary. They felt the message had to be changed. And we have seen that plan played out over and over again in Western Christianity, and it is an utter dead end. The Pastoral Epistles will show you why it's a dead end.

---

[2]This concern animates his famous *On Religion: Speeches to its Cultured Despisers* (*Über die Religion: Reden an die Gebildeten unter ihren Verächtern*, 1799, 1806, 1833).

Modern Evangelicalism:
Our Methods Must Change

The second error is that of modern evangelicalism. It basically says the church can't be built, the church won't effectively engage its culture, unless our methods are changed. The "key" to the advance of the gospel, in other words, is identified as methodology. Generally, there is little to no theological reflection on this methodology, and the methods deployed are insufficiently related to the gospel itself or to sound biblical theology.

The problem here is not creativity. It actually requires more creativity, not less, to minister biblically in one's culture. The problem is that modern evangelicalism in general has insufficiently contemplated method in relation to the gospel and theology while it has been overconfident in methods (in abstraction from the power of the Word and Spirit).

For instance, in looking at the succession of methodologies that have been hailed as the next new "key" to church growth over the last fifty years, we can make these three observations. First, evangelicals have typically treated methodology as if it is utterly neutral, having no effect upon the message (but it is not, and to think so is naïve). Second, evangelicals have spent precious little time asking what methodology is consistent with our theology. Third, we have not insisted that our methodology flow from our theology and from the gospel itself.

Modern evangelicals have, in general, acted as if the medium has no effect on the message and as if all methods are equally serviceable for gospel-ministry. In other words, you can take the message and send it out any way you want without impinging upon the content, and almost any method is conducive to producing the ends contemplated in gospel-ministry.

The Message Is the Method, and the Message Informs the Method

But the Pastorals constantly press you to see that how we do ministry is related to the message. Methodology is related to theology. The message and our methods are connected. Indeed, our methods must flow out of and be consistent with our theology and the gospel itself.

If in our message we are committed to a God who speaks infallible truth—to a sovereign God, to supernaturalism and the work of the Spirit—yet we adopt a methodology that embraces epistemic skepticism, consumerism, and materialism, then our methods will positively undermine the message that we're attempting to convey to the world.

To say it yet another way—if we are calling people to come to Christ, deny themselves, take up their cross, and die daily and we adopt a methodology to "bring them in" that says "have it your way," then our methods will utterly contradict our message. Our methodology will trump our theology. They will learn our real theology from our methodology rather than from our formal theology, which is not expressed in or consistent with our methodology (however sincerely we may hold to that theology and however concerned we may be to convey it).

In other words, our mode of disciple-making is inherently theological. The only question is whether that mode is consistent with and flows from our expressed theology or whether it is consistent with and expresses some other theology that is inconsistent with our own. James Montgomery Boice used to say, "What you win them by, you win them to." That is, our methods do matter. They teach our would-be disciples what we really believe. And they are influential on the nature and quality of discipleship that will be produced in those that respond to our ministry. Thus, our methods must be consistent with our theology, or they will undermine the very theology we want to commend and convey.

Contextualization: Traditionalists and Progressives

When we think about contextualization (and we all have to because we all have to do ministry situated in a culture), we will not merely ask, "What does this culture like or believe or think or prefer or esteem?" and then give them what they want. Nor will we start with the culture's assumptions and then move to the Scripture, attempting to find a point of contact that will meet our culture's approval.

Both "traditionalists" and "progressives" go wrong here. Some traditionalists tend to assume their inherited culture and then impose their assumptions on their methodology. Some progressives tend to adopt the culture and then impose their adoption of the culture in their methodology.

Neither of those approaches is correct. Such traditionalism often reinforces an ossified expression of theology contextualized in culture. This is usually a past cultural moment, typically identified by the traditionalist as an ideal or golden era. The progressive approach can tend to justify faddish, ever-changing methods that are inadequately theologically grounded. But we want neither a petrified traditionalism nor a protean progressivism.

Here is where the Pastorals help us. They teach us that God has given us a gospel-message and gospel-means, and our methodology must always flow out of and be related to that message and those means. Yes, we need creativity. But that creativity needs to be anchored in, connected to, and consistent with our theology. In other words, theology informs methodology (this is universally and inescapably true), and therefore our methodology ought to be deliberately and self-consciously derived from and consistent with our theology. This plays out in the Pastoral Epistles, so the Pastorals help us with both of those errors that have beleaguered the Western church for two hundred years.

The Gospel-Message and Gospel-Means Inform Our Methods

The Pastorals show us that God will build his church and that he has given us a gospel-message and gospel-means by which it is to be built. Our methods are to flow out of and are to be connected to that message and those means.

WHAT CAN WE LEARN FROM THE END OF THIS PERSONAL LETTER?

As we approach the end of this little correspondence, you may be asking yourself, "What can we learn about the gospel and grace and ministry from concluding comments in a personal pastoral letter like 2 Timothy?" That's a good question, and I'd like to briefly offer a three-part answer.

What can we learn about God and godliness, about Christian life and ministry from closing personal comments in a letter from Paul to Timothy? A lot. Can Paul show us the gospel in closing remarks, personal exhortations, requests, and words of greetings? Yes, he can. Are we to believe that we can learn of God's grace in this string of final thoughts? Yes, we are.

Inspiration

First of all, we believe in inspiration. You've just read a tremendous message from Bryan Chapell that dealt with the text in which the apostle Paul says *all* Scripture is given by inspiration and is profitable. That includes the censuses in Numbers and the genealogies in 1 Chronicles. It includes every part of the Bible. It is not all applicable in the same way, but it is all profitable and inspired. And so there's no part of God's Word from which we should expect not to be profited and instructed—including the ends of pastoral letters.

Personal and Public

Second, we should expect to learn about God, the gospel, the Christian life, and ministry from the end of this Pastoral Epistle because it is essentially a public letter. Yes, it is very personal, even more personal than 1 Timothy. But it's still a public letter. The towering early twentieth-century New Testament scholar J. Gresham Machen points this out in his work on the Pastorals. These letters, he observed, though they were personal, were always written with the congregation in view.[3]

Let me give you an example. Do you remember Mark Driscoll telling us how kind it was of the apostle Paul to do the name-naming in the letter instead of making Timothy do that? It was Paul who names Hymenaeus and Philetus (2:17). Paul was the one who names them as the heretics so that Timothy didn't have to. But how did the congregation find that out? Let me allow my imagination to run for a moment. Timothy stands up on Sunday morning in a house in Ephesus and says, "Three days ago I received a letter from Paul, the man who brought so many of you to faith in Jesus Christ, the man who is the planter of this congregation, its first pastor, a man who is my father in the Lord and who is among the apostles of the church. I received a letter from him. I have read it seventeen times in the last three days, and now I'm going to read it to you." And as he reads through the letter, he gets to the point where Paul says, "But avoid

---

[3] J. Gresham Machen, *The New Testament: An Introduction to Its Literature and History* (Carlisle, PA: Banner of Truth, 1976), 180.

irreverent babble, for it will lead people into more and more ungodliness, and their talk will spread like gangrene. Among them are Hymenaeus and Philetus, who have swerved from the truth, saying that the resurrection has already happened. They are upsetting the faith of some" (2:16–18).

It's in the public reading of the letter that the congregation learns of Paul's pronouncement. It is in Timothy's reading of Paul's personal letter out loud in the church service that the people hear the verdict. So it is not Timothy versus Hymenaeus and Philetus. He simply conveys the judgment of Paul. Can you imagine the reaction of the congregation? "Paul said that? Paul said that their teaching had gone astray from the truth and is like gangrene? Well clearly, then, we must avoid them and count them false teachers. No further questions. This is not just Timothy's opinion. This is an apostolic assessment that they have departed from the faith." So, yes, these letters are incredibly personal, but they are also public letters. They are meant to be read publicly to instruct, encourage, and edify the church. And that means the end of these letters will do the same thing.

Incidental Instruction

Third, in these closing remarks we're going to find what you might call *incidental instruction*. The first and the last part of these closing remarks give us rather direct applications of the truths that are being propounded in them. The final part of this letter begins with an exhortation, and it ends with a benediction. Their applications are clear and straightforward. But between that exhortation and benediction are requests, warnings, and greetings that are very personal and specific. You might ask, "How you can apply those to Christians in general?" Underneath the requests, warnings, and greetings are revealed commitments and truths that we can discern and from which we can learn.

Let me give you an example. If you are reading through Calvin's *Institutes* and you get to his treatment of prayer, not a few paragraphs into it he pauses to give you encouragements to prayer. As you read them, you are not only helped by Calvin's explicit, practical encouragements, but you're also helped by this thought as you read that section—"Calvin would not have written this if he didn't need these encouragements himself." And then it dawns on you that Calvin himself needed encouragement in his practice of prayer, just like you. It is not that Calvin had heard of a man in Silesia who once needed encouragement in prayer. No, the reason that he's giving you those practical exhortations is because he's had to struggle; he himself knows the struggle of prayer, and he wants to help other Christians. So you are helped by learning something that is incidental to the explicit point of Calvin's passage on prayer.

In a similar way, you will learn from Paul in this passage. His exhortation or request or warning may be explicitly and specifically directed toward Timothy, but underneath it there is a blessing waiting for you. There is a truth about the Christian life meant for your encouragement.

EXPOSITION: PAUL'S FINAL MESSAGE TO TIMOTHY (AND US)

Our passage outlines fairly straightforwardly:

1. Exhortation (4:6–8)
2. Requests (4:9–13)
3. Warnings (4:14–18)
4. Greetings (4:19–21)
5. Benediction (4:22)

For I am already being poured out as a drink offering, and the time of my departure has come. I have fought the good fight, I have finished the race, I have kept the faith. Henceforth there is laid up for me the crown of righteousness, which the Lord, the righteous judge, will award to me on that Day, and not only to me but also to all who have loved his appearing.

Do your best to come to me soon. For Demas, in love with this present world, has deserted me and gone to Thessalonica. Crescens has gone to Galatia, Titus to Dalmatia. Luke alone is with me. Get Mark and bring him with you, for he is very useful to me for ministry. Tychicus I have sent to Ephesus. When you come, bring the cloak that I left with Carpus at Troas, also the books, and above all the parchments. Alexander the coppersmith did me great harm; the Lord will repay him according to his deeds. Beware of him yourself, for he strongly opposed our message. At my first defense no one came to stand by me, but all deserted me. May it not be charged against them! But the Lord stood by me and strengthened me, so that through me the message might be fully proclaimed and all the Gentiles might hear it. So I was rescued from the lion's mouth. The Lord will rescue me from every evil deed and bring me safely into his heavenly kingdom. To him be the glory forever and ever. Amen.

Greet Prisca and Aquila, and the household of Onesiphorus. Erastus remained at Corinth, and I left Trophimus, who was ill, at Miletus. Do your best to come before winter. Eubulus sends greetings to you, as do Pudens and Linus and Claudia and all the brothers.

The Lord be with your spirit. Grace be with you. (2 Tim. 4:6–22)

Paul is saying to Timothy over and over again in this letter (as John Piper taught us), "Timothy, keep on feeding the white-hot flame of God's gift in you, namely, unashamed courage to speak openly of Christ and to suffer well for the gospel." And Paul does not cease with that instruction even in his concluding comments. All that he's said is designed to buttress Timothy in the race that he is running. So I want to draw attention to these five things: this exhortation, these requests, these warnings, these greetings, and the benediction. I want you to see how they all serve to buttress that message that Paul unveils in the first twelve verses of the letter.

Exhortation (4:6–8): Cross the Finish Line

For I am already being poured out as a drink offering, and the time of my departure has come. I have fought the good fight, I have finished the race, I have kept the faith. Henceforth there is laid up for me the crown of righteousness, which the Lord, the righteous judge, will award to me on that Day, and not only to me but also to all who have loved his appearing.

Paul's exhortation in 4:6–8 is very straightforward. Connect the end of 4:5 to 4:7 and you'll see it. "Fulfill your ministry," for "I have fought the good fight and finished the race." Do you see what Paul is motivating Timothy to faithfulness with? The finish line and Paul's own proximity to it.

He says, "Timothy, I'm about to cross the finish line. You cross the finish line, too." The application of that is pretty straightforward, isn't it? The Getty and Townend hymn, "O Church Arise," is all about it. It points you back to saints who've run the race well, but it points you forward to an assembly of saints who are awaiting you at the finish line.

> So Spirit, come, put strength in ev'ry stride,
> Give grace for ev'ry hurdle,
> That we may run with faith to win the prize
> Of a servant good and faithful.
> As saints of old still line the way,
>
> Retelling triumphs of His grace,
> We hear their calls and hunger for the day
> When, with Christ, we stand in glory.

And here's the apostle Paul saying to Timothy, "I've run the race; now I can see the end. It's days, it's months away. I've run the race; you run the race, and you cross the finish line, too. Your goal is nothing short of that finish line. There's no aim in ministry, there's no temporary or temporal success, there's no earthly satisfaction short of that finish line that will do. Cross the finish line."

Paul is saying to Timothy, "Do ministry with your eye on the finish line." Think of the last day as William W. How wrote, when "from Earth's wide bounds and oceans' farthest coasts through gates of pearl, stream the countless hosts singing to Father, Son, and Holy Ghost, hallelujah, hallelujah, and the King of Glory passes on his way."

Paul is saying to you all, "Think of that when you do ministry! That's the arena in which you're doing ministry; that's your ultimate goal. Yes, you want to do good now; you want to see people come to faith in Christ; you want to see people's lives transformed; you want to see the church grow and mature; you want to see communities totally changed; you're ready to pour yourself out, just like God has poured me out, to see that happen now, but that's not your finish line."

A number of years ago, there were a number of significant moral failures in the ministry among Reformed evangelicals in Britain. It deeply unsettled many of the brethren who were trying to do faithful, gospel-work there because some their heroes had fallen along the way. During this time, Geoff Thomas, who has been the pastor for almost a half-century of the Alfred Place Baptist Church in Aberystwyth, Wales, said to my dear friend and colleague Derek Thomas, "Derek, when I was a young man first going in the ministry, I wanted to do something great, but now I just want to cross the finish line." Pastor Thomas, reflecting on heroes falling all around him, longed to cross the finish line without shaming God's people and abandoning his Lord. He wanted to finish well. He didn't want to fall short of the goal.

And here's Paul saying to Timothy, I can see the finish line from where I am. I'm almost there. By God's grace, I've made it. You make it, too, Timothy. It helps us to have the testimony of saints who've run a long race and then to hold before us the picture of where it is that we're trying to get so that we get there, too. We need to exhort one another in this way, friends. The world and the flesh and the devil on every side want us to fall short of that finish line. And here's Paul exhorting his son in the Lord, "By God's grace I've gotten there; you get there, too."

The point of the exhortation is simple and clear but profound—to be a gospel-minister is to have yourself poured out by God as a drink-offering for the sake of the gospel. To be a gospel-minister is a hard fight and a long race. Be poured out. Fight the fight. Finish the race. Cross the finish line. Do so with Paul's example in mind and God's prize before your eyes.

Requests (4:9–13): Come Soon, with the Books and Cloak and Companionship

> Do your best to come to me soon. For Demas, in love with this present world, has deserted me and gone to Thessalonica. Crescens has gone to Galatia, Titus to Dalmatia. Luke alone is with me. Get Mark and bring him with you, for he is very useful to me for ministry. Tychicus I have sent to Ephesus. When you come, bring the cloak that I left with Carpus at Troas, also the books, and above all the parchments.

These requests are fascinating, aren't they? They boil down to this—"Timothy, I'm lonely, having been abandoned by most, and I'm cold now and need my cloak (or I will be when winter comes), and I'm unable to study without my books, especially

the parchments. Would you come see me soon (before winter-
time [see 4:21]) and bring them?" There is a lot here to meditate
upon—Mark's restoration to fellowship in ministry with Paul,
Paul's abandonment by Demas, Paul's unselfish dispatching of
others to points all over Asia Minor, etc. But I want to lock in
on the books. Many of you know Spurgeon's famous sermon on
this passage. Here's what the Prince of Preachers says about the
request "bring the books, especially the parchments":

> We do not know what the books were about and we can only
> form some guess as to what the parchments were. Paul had a few
> books, perhaps wrapped up in that cloak and Timothy was to be
> careful to bring them. *Even an apostle must read.* Some of our
> very ultra Calvinistic brethren think that a minister who reads
> books and studies his sermon must be a very deplorable specimen
> of a preacher. A man who comes up into the pulpit, professes to
> take his text on the spot, and talks any quantity of nonsense, is
> the idol of many. If he will speak without premeditation, or pre-
> tend to do so, and never produce what they call a dish of dead
> men's brains—oh! That is the preacher. How rebuked are they by
> the apostle! He is inspired, and yet he wants books! He has been
> preaching at least for thirty years, and yet he wants books! He
> had seen the Lord, and yet he wants books! He had had a wider
> experience than most men, and yet he wants books! He had been
> caught up into the third heaven, and had heard things which it was
> unlawful for a man to utter, yet he wants books! He had written
> the major part of the New Testament, and yet he wants books!
> The apostle says to Timothy and so he says to every preacher,
> "Give thyself unto reading." The man who never reads will never
> be read; he who never quotes will never be quoted. He who will
> not use the thoughts of other men's brains, proves that he has no
> brains of his own. Brethren, what is true of ministers is true of all
> our people. You need to read. Renounce as much as you will all
> light literature, but study as much as possible sound theological
> works, especially the Puritanic writers, and expositions of the
> Bible. We are quite persuaded that the very best way for you to be
> spending your leisure, is to be either reading or praying. You may

get much instruction from books which afterwards you may use as a true weapon in your Lord and Master's service. Paul cries, "Bring the books"—join in the cry.[4]

I trust that we all feel the force of Spurgeon's observations and his powerful rhetoric. If Paul was learning, reading, studying, and writing to the very end, surely we ought to be doing the same. Ministers of the gospel are, or ought to be, lifelong students.

Note what Paul asks for here. First, he asks for Timothy to come see him. He tells him that only Luke is with him, but he asks Timothy to bring Mark. My imagination wants to run wild. When these three are united in one place, you have half of the Gospel authors and the writers of over half of the New Testament. And if Timothy does what Paul says, when they are together they will also have along some books and special parchments that Paul thinks are particularly needful. Your mind can run with what's going to go on when they gather. I don't know, but I do know this—Paul knows that he's going to die in a matter of weeks or months, and he is still thinking about reading, learning, and leaving a deposit of sound truth in writing for the edification of the church.

This is hugely instructive for us in a day when so many are impatient of propositional truth and "logocentrism" and warn of "bibliolatry." When people belittle this book that you hold and preach from, they are belittling the product of a man who saw Jesus, a man who was brought into the ministry by Jesus. And they're belittling the pattern of Jesus. Isn't it amazing to you that when Jesus is on the road to Emmaus with the two discouraged disciples, he takes them to the Hebrew Bible? Jesus is there; couldn't he just *ad lib* it? No, he takes them to the Bible.

---

[4]Charles H. Spurgeon, "Paul—His Cloak and His Books," No. 54, November 29, 1863.

Some argue that the expositional preaching of the Bible is just about information-transfer, that postmodernists are beyond that now, and that it doesn't work that way anymore. But you need to reflect on Jesus' use of the book and Paul's devotion to the study of the Word and his concern to leave a written deposit of truth for the edification of the church.

Why did Paul think this was so important? Because he believed that the reading and hearing of the Word of God is a means of grace. And the preaching of that same Word is a means of grace. It is the way God gathers and perfects the saints. So when the faithful preacher rightly handles the Word of God, God himself delivers through the preacher his message into the hearts of God's people to teach them about himself, his grace, his gospel, and their godliness, and to facilitate a divinely word-mediated encounter with himself. In other words, the Word (written, read, and preached) is not just about information-transfer. It's not about filling their brains up with stuff. It's about bringing us into the presence of God. Paul knew that, and he's devoted to working on that to the end of his life.

Again, this point is clear (though we could have said much more about this glorious passage)—a gospel-minister reads, studies, learns, writes, and ministers until death, and the Word of God is a necessary means of grace and growth.

Warnings (4:14–18): Beware Opposition; Prepare for Abandonment; Know that the Lord Will Stand by You

Alexander the coppersmith did me great harm; the Lord will repay him according to his deeds. Beware of him yourself, for he strongly opposed our message. At my first defense no one came to stand by me, but all deserted me. May it not be charged against them! But the Lord stood by me and strengthened me, so that through me the message might be fully proclaimed and all the Gentiles might hear it. So I was rescued from the lion's mouth. The Lord will rescue me from every evil deed and bring me safely into his heavenly kingdom. To him be the glory forever and ever. Amen.

Again, the warnings here are very straightforward. "Timothy, watch out for Alexander, and don't be surprised if you find yourself all alone." But the assurances are stunning. "The Lord stood by me." The Lord rescued me "from the lion's mouth." "The Lord will rescue me. . . ." Clearly, Paul is trying to strengthen Timothy for the opposition that he will face by reminding Timothy of Paul's own opposition and travails and also the Lord's presence with Paul in his hour of need.

But there is a special phrase in this passage that I do not want you to miss. It's Paul's description of his first hearing. It is amazing—and one of the darkest passages in all of the Scripture. Have you missed it before? Paul says, "At my first defense, no one supported me, but all deserted me. May it not be counted against them!" (4:16, translation mine).

You know what stuns me about that? Paul had been left absolutely alone in the very culminating hour of his whole life and ministry. My insides want to explode at the thought of this. All I can think of is all the people who aren't named in this passage who weren't with the apostle Paul, but who should have been. This is *Paul*, for crying out loud. And he's alone in the end like his Lord. What's the subtext of that? What do we learn from that?

Do you hear what Paul is saying to Timothy (and to you) in recounting this? Paul is saying that being faithful in gospel-ministry doesn't mean that you are not going to be left alone, abandoned, deserted, forsaken. Your Master was left alone. All his disciples deserted him. And Paul, too, was left alone. No one was with him when he finally had the opportunity to give that defense and declare his faith. No one was with him.

You know, there is a whole generation of young preachers serving the church today with a fire in their bellies for the gospel. But they are deeply wounded by the church, and they're angry with the church because the church has let them down and the church has abandoned them and deserted them and left them alone, and they're angry with the church. You know, it's hard to love someone that you're angry with, that you're bitter toward. And these servants are bitter because they expected the church to be there for them and to not let them down in their time of need. But they were let down.

Well, here's the apostle Paul saying, "I love the church, and she wasn't there for me. She wasn't there for Jesus, and he loved her anyway and I love her anyway. May it not be counted against her. Because let me tell you this, Timothy, the Lord stood by me."

God may be calling you right into that, brothers, and when he does, he's not doing something singular and unprecedented and never seen before. It is exactly what happened to Paul. It is exactly what happened to your Savior. Why should you expect that if it happened to the Master, it won't happen to you, his disciples? Here Paul is saying, "Timothy, don't think that your faithfulness will mean that you won't be left alone, because you may be. But that is okay, because the Lord stood by me."

THE GOSPEL

Now, it's in this little warning section in 4:14–18 that Paul gets to the gospel. Paul says to Timothy (and to us), "Let me tell you what happened when I was left alone in the high court that day." And the heartbreaking thing is that no Christian but Paul himself saw or heard what he is about to describe—his culminating public proclamation of the gospel in the most intimidating and important of circumstances. Paul testifies that the Lord strengthened him so that through him "the proclamation might be fully accomplished, and that all the Gentiles might hear" (4:17, NASB).

What message, what proclamation is he talking about? He's already told you—the gospel. Take a look at 2 Timothy 1:8, where Paul speaks of "the gospel according to the power of God (NASB)." And what is the content of that gospel-message and proclamation? The next verses tell you. God "has saved us and called us with a holy calling, not according to our works, but according to His own purpose and grace which was granted us in Christ Jesus from all eternity, but now has been revealed by the appearing of our Savior Christ Jesus, who abolished death and brought life and immortality to light through the gospel, for which I was appointed a preacher and an apostle and a teacher" (1:9–11, NASB).

This is a thumbnail sketch of Paul's gospel-proclamation. And he offers these kinds of brief, pithy summarizations of the gospel constantly. They populate his letters. So, for instance, you can go back to 1 Timothy 2:3–6, where Paul speaks of "God our Savior, who desires all people to be saved and to come to the knowledge of the truth. For there is one God, and there is one mediator between God and men, the man Christ Jesus, who gave himself as a ransom for all, which is the testimony given at the proper time." And he then says that this message is for what he was appointed as a preacher (1 Tim. 2:7).

So that is the message that he proclaimed. He got to proclaim the gospel. That is what he had always longed to do. He prayed, "Lord, I want to proclaim the gospel in the precincts of the palace of the emperor in the heart of the city of Rome; get me there."

Now one point of this warning section is clear—faithfulness

in gospel-ministry is no guarantee that people will not oppose you and that fellow Christian workers won't abandon you. Paul is saying to Timothy, "I got to do it. I was alone. Everybody had deserted me, but I got to proclaim the gospel, and I not only proclaimed the gospel, which is the power of God, but I proclaimed the gospel that is the power of God *by the power of God.*" Go back to 2 Timothy 4:17 again and look at how he says that. "The Lord was there. The Lord stood by me. The Lord enabled me. The Lord strengthened me. He made me able to do this." Can you imagine what an intimidating context that would have been in which to proclaim the gospel? Paul is in this arena where everything's conspiring against him to mute the proclamation of the gospel; he's all alone, and yet he says, "Timothy, by the strength of God, I proclaimed the gospel there. It's what I'd always wanted to do."

Greetings (4:19–21): Salute the Saints

> *Greet Prisca and Aquila, and the household of Onesiphorus. Erastus remained at Corinth, and I left Trophimus, who was ill, at Miletus. Do your best to come before winter. Eubulus sends greetings to you, as do Pudens and Linus and Claudia and all the brothers.*

Here is one of those sections where we get incidental instruction. The exhortation is simple: "Timothy, I want you to greet some very special people for me, and I want you to send some greetings from some very special people to some other very special people." Paul spends a lot of time at the ends of his letters giving greetings. Is he just following the niceties of his day? I don't think so. What do we learn from this? We learn from this that Paul loves God's people in such a way that he wants to express that love. Conveying the love of Christians to Christians in such a way creates real and deep gospel-community.

There is an agenda in Paul's greetings and salutations, in his passing along of personal remarks to people—he wants to build up the body of Christ—its coherence, its communion—and he wants to do it by the expression of love. It is not something incidental and formal for him. He's not merely following custom. He's got an agenda in mind. He genuinely loves God's people; he wants God's people to know that he loves them; and he wants God's people to know that God's people genuinely love them.

Do you know how strengthening it can be to pass on that kind of word of commendation and greeting from brothers to brothers who aren't with one another? When we're not with one another in ministry (because we ministers are temperamentally paranoid), we're suspicious of one another. We're certain about ourselves, but that guy over there, we're not so sure about. And watch Paul, he does this with whatever you want to call it—the conservative party and the progressive party in the early church. He's constantly saying, "Okay, now we who are thought to be on the progressive wing are going to send a gift back to the traditionalists in Jerusalem. We want them to know that we love them and we care about them, even though they're, frankly, a little suspicious of what we're doing here in Asia Minor."

And he sends greetings for the same reason—he's building love and gospel-community in the body of Christ. That doesn't just happen. That kind of unity, brothers and sisters, doesn't just happen. It is done on purpose. In a letter of the New Testament, Paul has time to deliver those words of greetings, and you should, too. And so surely one thing we learn from this section is this—the gospel-minister cares about and loves people (and greets and passes along greetings) with a deliberate intentionality to contribute to the creation of gospel-community.

Benediction (4:22): The Blessing of God's Presence
and Grace

The Lord be with your spirit. Grace be with you.

This benediction is not to be missed (nor should any benediction be missed or taken for granted!). For many Christians, benedictions are like the memorized speech a flight attendant repeats in a nasal monotone before takeoff. What do frequent travelers do when the flight attendant (or video) begins to go over the standard instructions we've heard a million times? We zone out. Well, that's how some people react to the benediction. They zone out. And they're missing something huge.

Paul says to Timothy and to you, "The Lord be with you." That is huge. It's connected with everything else that he has said in this letter and everything else he said in his ministry. Remember that in Exodus 33, after the golden calf, God comes to Moses and says, "Okay, Moses, I've heard you. I'm not going to blast Israel into oblivion right here in the middle of the wilderness, but here's what I'm going to do. I'm going to send you on up to Canaan, but I'm not going to go with you." Very frankly, most of us would say, "Great deal. That's good. That'll work. We get to go to the Promised Land; we don't have to worry about getting the Lord mad because he's not in our midst anymore. That sounds good to me. Good deal." Do you remember what Moses says? "Lord, if you won't go with us, just go ahead and get it over right here because the whole thing that I'm about is being with you. The very essence of your grace is that you would be my God and I would be your person and that you would be Israel's God and that Israel would be your people. So if you're not going up with us, just kill us here. Let's just get it all over with right now." The Lord responds to the mediator's prayer and says, "I've heard you, and I will go up in your midst."

Paul is saying, "Timothy, the Lord will be with you." In the garden, after Adam and Eve sinned, God said, "Go. Go out of my presence. Go out of my fellowship. Go out of the enjoyment of communion and fellowship with me. Go out. Go!" And by grace, every time you hear a scriptural call to worship, do you know what God is saying to you? He's saying, "Come. Come into my presence; gather my people." If you speak the scriptural call to worship, you've already preached the gospel at the beginning of the worship service because it's not God's word "go." It's God's word "come." "Come unto me all my people and I will give you rest." "Come, worship, and bow down. Kneel before the Lord your Maker." "I'll fellowship with you. Come be with me; I'll be with you." And then when the benediction comes at the end, it's "go." But it's not "go away from me." It's "I will go with you. My presence with you isn't ending at the end of the service." Here's Paul saying to Timothy, "The Lord will be with you."

Frankly, Timothy and all in ministry need to know this desperately. We need to know and feel the presence of the Lord. With us. Standing by us. And Paul, who knew that experientially, pronounces this most precious of benedictions on us.

What are his last words? Grace. "Grace be with you." Because how is Timothy going to cross the finish line? How is he going to cope with being abandoned in faithful gospel-ministry? How is he going to deal with the opposition of Alexander? How is he going to deal with his own personal timidity? Not with his own resources but with the grace of God. Grace. His favor.

"Timothy, what you need to finish is something that doesn't come from within you; it comes from without you and is bestowed on you and is granted to you freely by the Lord. Grace. His saving favor. Utterly undeserved, but freely given, despite our demerit, at the cost of God's own Son. That's what you need, Timothy, if you are going to meet me on the other side of the finish line."

The benediction-comforts are clear—the gospel-presence of the Lord is the gospel-minister's one certain comfort, and God's grace is his one source of strength to fulfill Paul's exhortations to faithful gospel-ministry.

Many of you have twenty, thirty, forty, fifty years of ministry before you, God willing. I don't know how many more years I have. By God's grace, I want to meet you on the other side of that finish line. So my prayer for you is that God's peace—not the peace of rest and ease in this present world and in our current condition, but that peace of and from God, that total well-being that only God can bestow and the communion that you have with God, by God's grace, that gives peace—that *that* peace would be with you, my brothers and sisters, today even when the world is falling around your ears, even when you are engaged in unremitting conflict with the world, flesh, and Devil, that *that* peace would be with you through God your Father and Jesus Christ your Lord, until the day breaks and the shadows flee away.

GENERAL INDEX

SCRIPTURE INDEX